Pursuing Peace

Discovering God's Peace
in a Stressful Life

J.E. Huckabee

WestBow
PRESS
A DIVISION OF THOMAS NELSON

WestBow Press books may be ordered through
booksellers or by contacting:

WestBow Press
A Division of Thomas Nelson
1663 Liberty Drive
Bloomington, IN 47403
www.westbowpress.com
1-(866) 928-1240

ISBN: 978-1-4497-8614-4 (sc)
ISBN: 978-1-4497-8613-7 (e)
ISBN: 978-1-4497-8615-1 (hc)
Library of Congress Control Number: 2013903254

Printed in the United States of America

WestBow Press rev. date: 2/22/2013

Contents

Acknowledgments

My deepest thanks go to all of those men and women who have taught me and freely given of themselves in this life to broaden my knowledge and wisdom.

To my wife Alice who continues to lovingly and patiently forgive me of my imperfections and holds my wing as we fly towards peace.

To all of the many people at West Bow Press who helped orchestrate this symphony of words – thank you.

The Axxiom Men's Group – you were the first step that God had me take to really get this book off the ground. To Andy Ramos, a great friend, and a warrior for Christ.

This would have been much more difficult without people like my mother Dee Dee Huckabee, my aunt Marcy Lytle (a great author), my uncle Jon Lytle, Willie Taylor and Pastor Mylon Avery (another great author). Thank you for taking the time out of your busy schedules to read some of my worst, unedited portions of the manuscript. Your feedback and encouragement along the way was so needed and appreciated.

To my Teacher, Guide, Healer, Forgiver and ever present Friend through it all – The Holy Spirit. Thank you for helping me put my heart's words onto paper. At times, it was exhausting. May it bring glory to your name, Jesus, as it enriches the lives of your children.

Introduction

It almost seems silly on the surface to think that a business executive, husband, and father of three could find the time to sit down and write a book, much less about peace. The essence of the word itself doesn't seem to fit as part of the equation. In fact, as I type this meek introduction to my first book, my five-year-old daughter stands on the stairs in our home telling her younger brother, "I just wanted to tell you that I am having a party right now at the bottom of the stairs."

Kids have this amazing ability to be at peace with life. They can literally shut out the world around them and create their own internal world. They utter strange but cute sounds with each step they take. They carry around their toys of comfort as they walk and sing the song of joy they made up, note by note.

Children keep things simple. Their perspectives are still shallow and untarnished by the world outside their homes. Decades of memories, trials, burdens, accomplishments, failures, bad choices, moments of déjà vu, and deep wounds covered by tough scars have not filled their minds. They are innocent, yes, but they are simple.

I have certainly learned one thing in twenty years of business, "Keep it simple, stupid (KISS)." This principle, which Lockheed engineer Kelly Johnson coined, was used in the design of the Blackbird jet airplane. The idea was to design the plane so an average mechanic with simple tools could service it while in the field of combat.

I may not have been in the military, but I served under my pappy as a young boy. He was a master sergeant in the US army who served in WWII, the Korean War, and the Army Reserves. A child of the Depression, he knew what it meant to get by with simple things. He applied the KISS principle for thirty-eight years as an advisory scientist for IBM and a fellow of the American Watchmakers-Clockmakers Institute. On the surface, he would seem like a complex man. But I knew from a child that his mind, though powerful, was built on simplicities. He was a man of simple principles, unwavering.

We all have a story to tell. Our upbringings and our careers construct the pieces of complexity that shape whom we are. The older we get, the more we tend to lose our childlike simplicity. Our life experiences begin to shape patterns in our minds that control the way we react to life's situations. And the way we react builds patterns that shape our emotions. And it is quite easy for human beings to begin to live their lives from emotion instead of principle.

With this said, you can imagine that a mind full of all of this stuff and surrounded by emotions could end in stress. It's no wonder so many books are in print about peace. A simple ISBN search on the word is mind-boggling in itself. So it seemed to me that, if the formula for stress were so simple, the formula for peace should be just as easy. I wish it were so. The concept certainly can be, but we get our wagon wheels stuck in life's proverbial mud in the process. "Go west, young man" sounds like a simple concept, but the process of doing it uncovers a tough road ahead.

When I set out to write this book, I wanted to look back at my own life, analyze the stuff, and compare notes on what worked and what failed to bring peace in my own life. I realized that people around me were burdened. They were quick to rationalize based on emotional responses to life. People were set off easily. They could smile one minute and scowl the next. They could praise God and use foul language in the same sentence. What a mess! And I could see the same traits in myself at times.

As I made my mental journey through my own life, it became apparent to me that things matched up. I began to build a formula that seemed to define the mess and denote a cure. I began to apply some of these things to my life and saw some pretty remarkable changes in myself. It almost seemed too easy at first. So I figured I better broaden the number of participants in my private study. I worked these principles with family members, friends, coworkers and business associates that I interacted with on a daily basis.

As I began to include others around me in this initiative, I found a similar transformation. People changed. I would inject these principles into the situations that came up in my career. I started to make my response to people's questions more focused on what brought peace to my own soul. Amazingly, most of all, as coworkers and friends would engage me for a response to a situation, I found them increasingly involved for a new answer to new concerns. And before long, I began to hear subtle yet appealing praise reports about things transpiring in their lives.

I noticed these fellow human beings were beginning to talk about positive things instead of negative ones. Coworkers were beginning to approach problems with a new attitude. Instead of dread for the problem, they began to, in its simplest form, take a divide-and-conquer approach to issues instead of dread and a complaining attitude. People around me were actually tasting the joys of peace and wanting more. It became addictive for them as well as me.

When you have spent a lot of time with a negative person, it is easy to see how his negative attitude can rub off on both you and others around you. It can suck the life right out of you. But when you see a negative person begin to smile and think positive, it will change your life and the lives of those around you. There is something powerful about seeing that transformation take place.

I continued to try myself with these principles. As I prayed about them, God began to show me that, if I could just put forth some effort, He would help me find peace. And as I assisted others with it, He began to speed things along. And I became convinced that peace had a formula built on simple, biblical concepts. And I wasn't about to let the progress I was seeing in the lives of those around me stop at the factory walls where I worked or in the homes of family and friends whose time I shared.

I desire the reader find this book as a stew of ingredients. I wanted to write in the simplest terms I could. I wanted to use language that laymen would feel comfortable with. It was important for me to mix some of my own life experiences with the strength of God's Word. In its greatest effect, I wanted this book to bring hope to all who read it. They too could find peace, regardless of their backgrounds, education, life experiences, or current situation.

Life without peace is a miserable journey. I pray you will become wide eyed to the simplicity of the principles in these pages. May you crack a smile with a tear of sorrow in your eye. I hope you can breathe deep the air of God's peace and apply the simple power of His Word to your life. May you ground your decisions in wisdom, and may their results yield a life full of vigor, passion, accomplishment, and meaning. And may you live the life of peaceful purpose that God designed for you before you were ever born.

In His Peace,

Jason

Foreword

Living a life of peace in a fallen world is impossible without God. No man, woman or child can go through life without being faced with the difficulties that this life gives. Nor are we immune from the consequences of our decisions. Peace is something that people long for. It is something that we can all partake of and something that Christ offers to all of us.

I wrote this book for two main reasons. First of all, I wrote it as a resounding message of hope to those struggling to find peace. The content within these ten chapters contains individual aspects of peace based on scripture and experiences from my life and career. As you read, breathe easy knowing that any of these principles can begin to bring peace into your life. I encourage you to read all the way through the book. Mark or highlight areas that you are interested in. When you are done, go back through and pick one or two principles and begin to apply them in your everyday life. Start slow. Rest calmly in the grace of our Lord. We're not perfect. But we can begin to enter the waters of peace through our actions and know that we are saved by grace and not by perfection.

Secondly, I wrote this as a challenge to the reader to venture into the ways of peace. In so doing, it is my sincere prayer that you would not only experience peace like never before, but that your relationship with Jesus Christ might grow stronger and more deeply. These principles take practice and time. This book can help as a manual for building peace into your life. Use it as a guide but never let it replace the solid platform of God's Holy Word. Keep your Bible close as you make progress with peace.

"For in Him we live, and move, and have our being." – Acts 17:27 (KJV)

Ah!, soul are you here without comfort and rest, Marching down the rough pathway of time? Make Jesus your Friend ere the shadows grow dark; O accept of this peace so sublime!

Peace, peace, wonderful peace, Coming down from the Father above! Sweep over my spirit forever, I pray In fathomless billows of love!

"Wonderful Peace" Hymn by Warren D. Cornell, 1889

In the beginning God created the heavens and
the earth. The earth was formless and empty, and
darkness covered the deep waters. And the Spirit of
God was hovering over the surface of the waters.

—Genesis 1:1–2 (NLT)

Secularized schools have begotten a secularized society.
The child is the father of the man and, if the child is led to
believe he is merely an evolved beast, the man he becomes
will behave as a beast, either aggressively struggling for
supremacy himself or blindly following aggressive leaders.

—Henry M. Morris, Scientific Creationism

Chapter 1

In the Beginning, God ...

The title of this chapter says it all. "In the beginning, God ..." You may ask, "What does that have to do with peace?" I struggled with the idea of peace when I realized the opposite fills this world. But I wasn't looking in the right place.

About a year ago, my wife and I took our kids to the park on a warm Saturday morning. We intended to just hang out, cook some hot dogs, and help my oldest son learn how to ride his bike. It was a nice day, a little on the warm side but nice nonetheless. The park was not very crowded at all, and we picked a nice spot to have our peaceful family picnic. As I began to fire up the grill, I felt a buzz in the air. Then we looked at each other as a prop plane came soaring over the tree line. It flew right over our heads and landed at the airport across from the park. The kids thought it was great. My face likely indicated that I saw it differently.

For starters, who in their right mind would put a nice park right next to an airport? Or rather, who in their right mind would go looking for peace at a park right next to an airport? Did this goofy decision lie with the park planner or the father who drove the minivan to the park that day? Debates like this have plagued humankind for thousands of years. Was it the chicken or the egg?

One could say that a great deal of our lack of peace comes from our own way of looking at life and not because of the events that unfold before us. I would like to think that God looks down through time, sees how we react to things, and asks why we make things so hard. Why do we try to analyze things as they play out? What could we have done to make them turn out better? Where could I go to make sure that I have a peaceful day with my kids? After all, my weekend with them is short enough as it is, so I should take the time to plan the best strategy, right?

Such thinking only muddies the waters of our souls. It gets our brains into a pattern of second-guessing our lives. Before long, we find we'll always be less pleased with the results of our lives and go looking for ways to make them better ... next time. This strategy is mind-deadening. And it takes away the soil of our souls that grows peace in our lives.

When I was younger, I tried to read through the Bible in a year. What is interesting to me now is that I always seemed to start at Genesis 1. And if there was anything that I did accomplish, it was reading that first verse countless times yet never finishing the book in that given year. I think I had "In the beginning" memorized by the time I got to Exodus.

Later in my life, I realized a great mystery and power in that first part. As I lay in bed one night, reveling in the mysteries of God, I thought of this passage in Genesis. My mind was stuck on the water part. "The earth was formless and empty, and darkness covered the deep waters" (Gen. 1:2 NLT).

As I lay on my back, staring into the dark, I imagined myself in this span of time in eons past. At first, I almost jumped out of bed. Picture the scene. You are floating on your back in the middle of an ocean of black. This ocean spans the entire surface of the earth. There are no mountains or continents. Just water. Let's just pretend that you could breathe. Remember, God has not yet created the earth's firmament. So there would be no oxygen to breathe yet! But suppose we could see while floating there.

I envisioned the most spectacular sky that humankind ever saw, a jet-black sky with no cloud cover or atmosphere to block what lay beyond. And what was visible beyond the black was an intense carpet of stars and no moonlight to drown them out.

I had to get a grip on myself because I don't like floating in water when I can't touch the ground beneath me. And I don't like to think about what could be beneath me and above the ground. Don't get me wrong. I like to fish, I like the ocean, and I like swimming in general. But the thought of floating in the earth's ocean of Genesis 1 somewhat freaked me out. Then I realized that there were no sharks yet in Genesis 1. "And the Spirit of God was hovering over the surface of the waters" (Gen. 1:2 NLT)

I remember the first time my kids got in the water on the beach in Florida. You would expect the response, "The water is cold!" I suspect the waters of Genesis 1 were probably pretty cold. There was no sun to warm them by day and no atmosphere to protect the surface from the cold chill of space. When our astronauts were working on the surface of the moon in decades past, there was little lunar atmosphere, and it was -290 degrees Fahrenheit in the shade. That should give you an idea of Genesis 1 water, just emptiness and cold. But then the Holy Spirit showed up on the scene, hovering over the face of the waters.

As I lay there, trying to warm up my thoughts and pulling the covers up to my chin, I fathomed the mystery of Genesis 1 and the absolute aloneness that must have existed without God. Had there been that much quiet in the park with my kids, I might have thought of it as peaceful. Yet this version of quiet did not give me a sense of peace at all. But when the Holy Spirit came along, my frozen, floating body began to thaw. I could feel His presence hovering over me. It was as if the warmth of a close friend thawed out my anguish and concerns.

I felt meaning and purpose, as I knew the Creator was about to do something amazing and spectacular. It was comfortable and exciting. And in an instant, I knew God was here to make a way in a cold and barren world where there seemed to be no approach. The present was shaping into a bright and shining future. As Horatio Spafford penned in the 1873 hymn, "It was well, with my soul."

I was assured in the knowledge that God was in control of things and He would make things right. But that's not the first part of Genesis 1. That was the second verse. Sometimes in life, our circumstances lodge our minds between verses one and two. We float in a cold, dead sea of doubt and anxiety. Our minds bounce around from left to right, firing off pulses of pain and emotion and stirring up the waters of our souls. We're wrecks. We can't think straight. We lack the one thing that brings us stability. "In the beginning God created the heavens and the earth" (Gen. 1:1 NLT, emphasis added).

So why would we have ever gotten to that point in the first place if we knew the first verse? Before the cold, dead sea came, there was God. And after the creation story played out, there was still God. He is on the scene from the beginning. So what are we afraid of? What are we concerned about? Where is our anchor? Who is in control of our lives, Him or us?

God's Greatest Creation

God really got down to business after the opening scene. He established the framework in His handiwork for what I call "decided movement." Up until this point, a movement from God birthed everything that He created. For example:

- one explosion bred stars.
- one star's movement collided with another and created other stars.
- galaxies were born.
- gas clouds were built.
- planets were birthed through intense crashes of semi-molten rock.

Everything new fed off something before it in a great cosmic chain reaction.

Then God created the land and sky. He filled that cold, dead ocean with living creatures that brought color and warmth to its waters. The great whales of the sea plotted their courses. God filled the sky with birds that chose to fly here and there. Herds of animals moved in all directions. Imagine the sounds that began to roar beneath the newly formed clouds.

Everything began to set off on its own course and live its own life, that is, to go where it would and do what it wished. Then God created people, the grand finale, the final scene, the best of the best. So what set humans apart from the rest of the noisemakers at the end of Genesis 1? God made humankind in His own image. He gave the human a soul, a destiny. He gave the first humans a choice and a chance at life beyond that of the oceans' algae.

You see, God had a plan. He made humanity for a relationship. He had a special purpose for people, and He equaled His purpose with the first man when God gave him a woman. It was all about relationship. It was centered around us and not I.

God intended to put people on earth to live in harmony with each other, that is, in relationship with each other and Him. He created what was supposed to be one big, happy family. And when He created us, the verse states He was quite pleased with us. "Then God looked over all He had made, and He saw that it was very good" (Gen. 1:31 NLT).

Choices

But what would real love be unless it was chosen? God didn't want to be a puppet master. He loved us too much for that. So He gave us a choice as to whether we would love Him back or not. Not only would He allow us to choose how we lived out our daily lives, He gave us the choice to follow after Him or after our own selfish desires. And with this choice came mankind's choice to disobey God's directives.

My kids like to get what they want. They think what they want is what is best for them. And they are not bashful at making it clear they want something. But I can assure you that what they want is not always what is best for them. You can imagine that, when I declare something they want as not good, there is some backlash. That inner part comes out, and with it comes their choice to react.

God knew this new world He created was perfect as it was and mankind would have everything they needed to have a wonderful, peaceful life. But He also knew that true love is a choice and He would give them the option. But He cautioned them that knowing the difference between good and evil would bring heartache, not peace. So as a good Father, He told them not to eat the fruit of the Tree of the Knowledge of Good and Evil (Gen. 2:17). Yet Adam and Eve made their choice to disobey. And with that choice came the rush of consequences that have plagued us ever since. "For I was born a sinner—yes, from the moment my mother conceived me" (Ps. 51:5 NLT). "When Adam sinned, sin entered the world. Adam's sin brought death, so death spread to everyone, for everyone sinned" (Rom. 5:12 NLT).

You and I, as the Bible states, are "born into sin." "For I was born a sinner—yes, from the moment my mother conceived me." (Psalm 51:5 NLT)

Thanks to Adam and Eve's choice to disobey God, we inherit what I call the "sin gene." I, my father, and my paternal grandfather have blue eyes. Essentially, we have the genes for blue eyes. Not everyone has blue eyes so not everyone received the genes for them. But everyone gets the "sin gene."

Now that we know we can and will sin (or do wrong in the sight of God), what does this do to a life with peace? It increases our risk of not having it. The whole idea of sinning brings degradation to God's perfect world that He gave us in Genesis 1. Adam and Eve's choice to disobey brought sin into the world and thus tarnished the life they handed down to their children and we now hand down to ours.

The smallest of sins and the largest, most horrific of sins leave consequences with them that shape society and prepare the future of the unborn. What was done in the past by choice has shaped the present we live in. The choices we make today will affect the futures of our children and their children. Choices have consequences. We'll discuss that more in chapter 3. But let me be clear, choosing this or that can have a profound effect on the level of peace in our souls. And when we are not at peace, we are primed for errors in judgment. And this too brings about more bad decisions. The process escalates and becomes a stagnant sewage of a life with no hope, purpose, and goals. The situation lends itself to a person who, as my dad says (describing an old motorcycle), is "rode hard and put up wet." In a situation like that, we're looking for a quick fix. And I'm not necessarily talking about drugs or alcohol, though that has been the lure of many, but I am speaking to the selfish desires that bring us a quick fix of happiness.

When we get to that point in life, we no longer care much about those around us. The original plan God had of relationship with Him and each other flies out the proverbial window. Now we only care about ourselves. When you live in a world of "Me, Me, Me," you surround yourself with people who don't want to have anything to do with you. You push yourself into a world of selfish motives and shallow desires. And you can forget relationships in a world like that.

If the garden of Eden were truly peaceful (which it was),

then it seems good sense to believe that the preceding world of "Me, Me, Me" must be clamorous. So we walk through life in a fog of despair. Our dreams have been replaced with idle sprints to quick drinks of muddy water. Our souls begin to reek of stingy, egocentric dross. What a pitiful way to live!

We all have bad days. But I'm speaking to a way of life here. Each of us finds ourselves, to a certain degree, somewhere along the level of "Me, Me, Me." Maybe we're just slightly along that dark and dingy road. Or maybe we've walked it so long that we're hopelessly lost in its dark forest of despair. In J.R.R. Tolkien's book, The Two Towers, Treebeard (or Sindarin) was the eldest of the Ents in the Fangorn forest. He was said to have a strong hatred for the evil orcs. Treebeard's roots had grown deep in complacency in the midst of his bad circumstances, and he was content with his pending doom. But two hobbits, Merry and Pippin, came along and convinced him to step out of the peaceless misery and take a stand. His choice made for a great comeback scene in Peter Jackson's movie.

I have observed something else under the sun. The fastest runner doesn't always win the race, and the strongest warrior doesn't always win the battle. The wise sometimes go hungry, and the skillful are not necessarily wealthy. And those who are educated don't always lead successful lives. It is all decided by chance, by being in the right place at the right time. (Eccl. 9:11 NLT)

Life is about change. Ecclesiastes 3 speaks of changing seasons. And with transformation can come difficult situations. It's just the way things go. When things hit us hard, we have to choose our reaction. We have to put our minds to a platform of thought, either stable or shaky. I have not always dealt with situations the best way in my life. I have placed my thoughts on unstable platforms and made poor decisions that bred additional misery down the road. And it all zapped my peace. But when difficult times come, if I am quick to recall that "In the beginning, God …" then I can reassure myself that He is in charge and, no matter what, I can be at peace.

I don't always like what life brings, but it is in harmony with God's original plan when I choose to place Him at the center of my life and to think of Him and others instead of myself. A mysterious yet powerful effect transpires when I do this. Peace. I encourage you to begin to do the same in your own life. Breed peace by your actions.

So God created human beings in His own image. In the image
of God He created them; male and female, He created them.

—Genesis 1:27

Then the Lord God formed the man from the dust of
the ground. He breathed the breath of life into the
man's nostrils, and the man became a living person.

—Genesis 2:7

So the Lord God caused the man to fall into a deep sleep.
While the man slept, the Lord God took out one of the man's
ribs and closed up the opening. Then the Lord God made
a woman from the rib, and he brought her to the man.

—Genesis 2:21–22

Chapter 2

Made in His Image

I used to believe that humankind was made in the image of God, but today somewhat changed that for me.

"Mommy, what day is today?" my youngest son asked his mother in a sort of sluggish, morning confusion.

With some hesitation and a lump in her throat, she simply replied, "Thursday."

"But why are we having cereal?" he replied.

You see, my kids eat cereal on Mondays and Fridays, but they get oatmeal in the middle of the week. The little guy was just trying to find out why he was getting cereal on a Thursday.

"Dalton doesn't want to go to school today because he's sad, so we're eating cereal."

I had to leave the room as I was finding it difficult to hold my composure as the man of the house. In the next thirty minutes, I would have to pick up our seventy-five-pound, nine-year-old German shepherd in my arms and take him to the vet. Only this day, he would not be coming home. Thor could not walk due to paralysis in his rear legs, which a genetic mutation brought on a disease called spinal myelopathy. The disease came on really fast. It started with a little limp on his walks. Then he slightly dragged his foot. Before long, he wore his back nails down until they bled and walks were now a thing of the past.

My trip home from work the day before was hectic. Thor could no longer walk, and he lay shaking at the back door as my wife and the kids walked in. He was distraught. He didn't know why he was having problems, and now he couldn't control his bowel movements. It was a tough night and an even harsher morning.

This hound met me at the back door when I got home from work for nine years with eyes wide, tongue out, ears back in reverence, and tail wagging side to side. He was so glad to see me home. And now, there would be no Mr. Grunts (as we called him) waiting for me at the door.

I was without peace this morning. I was hurting. I was a wreck. And I prayed the whole way to the vet, "God, give me peace. Give me peace. Strengthen me. Hold onto me."

"Do not be anxious about anything, but in every situation, by prayer and petition, with thanksgiving, present your requests to God. And the peace of God, which transcends all understanding, will guard your hearts and your minds in Christ Jesus" (Phil. 4:6–7 NIV).

I can't vouch for souls, but I can tell you that I felt that sweet spirit of my loving dog leave his body on his last, deep breath as he left this earth. I'm not sure where it went, but I know it didn't stay in that pitiful circumstance that he was embodied in. I made sure he was at peace at the end, but amazingly, God, in the ninth hour of my ordeal, grabbed my heart and fulfilled His promise to guard it from the toughest pain I was sure I would feel. He stepped in after a short burst of spiritual strengthening and "anointed my head with oil." He pulled out the roots of anxiety, and I thanked Him for it, all the way home with eyes full of tears.

Undoubtedly, we are made in God's image. He said it. I believe it. There are things He didn't say as well. But that doesn't mean it's not real. The love, the genuine affection that our sweet Thor had for each one of us and everyone he met, was of God. I believe God made him for us. He made him to love us no matter what. And through the pain of losing him, God allowed yet another lesson of peace to unfold. Our dog showed us a slice of God's pure love for us, no matter what. "The secret things belong unto the Lord our God; but those things which are revealed belong unto us and to our children for ever, that we may do all the words of this law" (Deut. 29:29 KJV).

Spinal disease in a canine, broken arms, car wrecks, lost jobs, divorce, wars, murder, or insulting words, none of it makes sense in the moment. Our world took a turn for the worse when Adam and Eve decided they would venture out into waters that God said would be troubled. So we deal with these things on an ever-coming basis. Sometimes, they are due to our own actions, other times, they are because of the actions of others, and occasionally, Mother Nature has a hand in it.

But God is certainly in control. He allows nothing that He will not use for good in our lives when we trust Him. This world may groan, but its God groans not. And His passion is a love for us. He created the things of this life and us to show us His love and comfort us among life's groans with His peace. And as we travel life's roads, we deal with its burdens. When we stick to God's promises, we can rest assured that He will teach us along the way. He will guide us and heal our wounds.

I never expected to be so emotionally taken by a dog. I grew up with these animals. I lost count years ago as to how many dogs I had growing up. In fact, I grew up with many German shepherds. But this was the first time I had one living in the house. Thor was with us from sunrise to sunset. He slept outside the door of our bedroom. He was truly a member of our family and our protector. His emotions and his character were woven into the fabric of our lives. And when we lost him, it hurt deeply.

But God's creatures were created for us. And I believe that God made Thor especially for us. Jesus formed his personality to fit us, and He ensured that, when He took him away, we would learn something special about His peace. "But the Counselor, the Holy Spirit-the Father will send Him in My name-will teach you all things and remind you of everything I have told you.

Peace I leave with you. My peace I give to you. I do not give to you as the world gives. Your heart must not be troubled or fearful" (John 14:26-27 HCSB).

People

People were indeed created in God's image. We certainly know what we look like. Though we come in all shapes and sizes, we clearly have solid similarities as people. The scriptures paint a picture of Christ's bodily image that shows a clear similarity. In the book of Revelation, Jesus is described in many aspects that are so closely resembling our own form—His body, hair, eyes, feet, voice, right hand, mouth, and countenance.

I turned around to see the voice that was speaking to me. And when I turned I saw seven golden lampstands, and among the lampstands was someone like a son of man, dressed in a robe reaching down to His feet and with a golden sash around His chest. The hair on His head was white like wool, as white as snow, and His eyes were like blazing fire. His feet were like bronze glowing in a furnace, and His voice was like the sound of rushing waters. In His right hand He held seven stars, and coming out of His mouth was a sharp, double-edged sword. His face was like the sun shining in all its brilliance. When I saw Him, I fell at his feet as though dead. Then He placed His right hand on me and said:

"Do not be afraid. I am the First and the Last." (Rev. 1:12–17 NIV)

Jesus Christ, the Son of God, looks like us. He came to this earth, and he was born of a virgin woman. He grew up like us. He endured the things of life that we do. As God Himself, He sinned not. He was perfect. Yet He experienced the lack of peace all around Him. He saw people experience things that robbed them of peace. People of this world are constantly being tried of the results of sin in a broken world. Some are trivial; others are more pressing.

A couple days after our dog died, I took my oldest son to the local pool for swimming lessons. I was still pretty down about the preceding days, but I was attempting to make light of a bad situation by watching my son flail like a fish. It was pretty warm that night, but the breeze over the cool water helped make me comfortable as I sat in my chair in the shade.

I had a nice view of my son until two ladies sat in front of me and blocked my view.

Wow. I quickly went from slight serenity to a quick moment of dissatisfaction and a bent mood of irritation.

Little did I know that, when I sat my smartphone on the edge of my chair, I had unknowingly prepared the next test of myself for peace. When I jumped up and pulled my chair to move it, my phone flew out of the chair. Worse, the impact it made on the corner as it struck the concrete and the sound of glass cracking really got me going.

It's those two ladies' fault! I thought. But was it really their fault, or was God using meager moments to get my attention and to teach me His lessons about peace?

The ladies in front of me were a part of this experience, my son in the pool played a hand, and my wife deciding we needed to have swim lessons in the first place, they all played a hand in the moment. And the boneheaded decision I so easily made to set my phone on the edge of my chair as I sat over a carpet of stone was the lit fuse to this life lesson.

About that time, I received an email from my dad that came in surprisingly to my phone. As I scraped the glass dust off the surface and read the message, I could see he had replied to an email I had sent him and Mom about our dog. I was brought me back down a notch, and as I gazed at the water, I saw a huge, blue moon popping right above the trees over the pool. It was about eight o'clock that evening, and the moon was out. And what a moon it was, absolutely huge and beautiful!

This is where readers find that the author has taken a bad situation and magically turned it shining in a few orchestrated words, all to prove a point. Well, this is real life after all. And sometimes God's finale for proving a point ends differently. That meager moment of mine didn't end simply with the huge blue moon and the sound of children's laughter. It ended when I recognized the message. He was giving me peace with the pain of feet covered in fire ants.

When I moved my chair, I set it down next to the grass, and my feet were sitting next to a mound of fire ants. And they had found their invader and ordered the attack on my ankles. These tiny insects came to the port of Mobile in Alabama in the 1930s aboard a South American cargo ship. Though an accident, they too became a part in the lessons of peace for me this summer evening.

We have to remember that we live in a fallen world. And creation itself groans because of man's sin. The earth was not meant to be like this. When people were created, we were placed in a garden of Eden where I believe fire ants were harmless. But when people changed the landscape of our relationship with God, so too did the landscape transform around people. And we bear the pains of that mural as nature groans.

> Against its will, all creation was subjected to God's curse. But with eager hope, the creation looks forward to the day when it will join God's children in glorious freedom from death and decay. For we know that all creation has been groaning as in the pains of childbirth right up to the present time. And we believers also groan, even though we have the Holy Spirit within us as a foretaste of future glory, for we long for our bodies to be released from sin and suffering. (Rom. 8:20–23 NLT)

As people, we groan. Nature groans. We lived together before the fall in peace. Now we groan and fight the results of sin in this world, and our life in peace now becomes a battle for peace. But when we reconsider the pain of the day, not as some happenstance but as an opportunity to learn of God's peace, we can see that God is there to bring good out of the bad situations. My phone still has cracked glass, but it now reminds me of that beautiful blue moon, my son winning the front crawl pool race, my dad's kind words of remembrance of my great dog, and the ant bites I know will not be awaiting me when I arrive in heaven one day and see my family who have passed on before me. Barefoot and carefree.

What can you do to promote world peace?
Go home and love your family.

—Mother Teresa

Friendship is born at that moment when one person says
to another: "What! You too? I thought I was the only one."

—C.S. Lewis

Do I not destroy my enemies when I make them my friends?

—Abraham Lincoln

Chapter 3

Family, Friends, and Acquaintances

I have learned over the years that there is a distinction between people: the people around us who we don't know and never meet, the people around us who consist of friends, and the people who are family. We'll start with the latter.

My mother's father (Papaw) was an amazing man. I called him on the phone when he was in a nursing home and close to the end of his life. His heart was beginning to fail him after years of surgeries. I wanted to check on him, to tell him that my wife was pregnant with our first child, and to say that the baby would be named Dalton after his father, Ralph Dalton. Needless to say, Papaw was thrilled. I was so sad to learn the news that he later died before our son could be born, but such is life. We don't set the timetables for God's teaching preparations. "How beautiful on the mountains are the feet of those who bring good news, who proclaim peace, who bring good tidings, who proclaim salvation"

(Isa. 52:7 NIV).

Papaw was an educated man. He was literally months away from his doctorate degree, and he was a minister. But God had plans for him, and Papaw would soon be traveling. From starting a church in Anchorage (where my Uncle Tim would be born) to a church in California (where my mother would be born) to the jungles of Central America, Papaw was on a mission to preach the gospel. And in the village of Frank's Eddy in the Cayo District of Belize, Central America, there would be no need for a PhD.

Papaw had more scriptures memorized than anyone I've ever known. He could commit whole chapters of the Bible to memory. He could sit there and recite an entire chapter of the Bible from memory while looking at you in the eyes. It was as if he were telling you a story and it went straight to your heart. He could answer your questions about life, look up the passages for you in the Word, and show you what God had to say about that. God made him for this.

His ministry in Belize was quite amazing. My grandparents lived in the jungle. Papaw designed and built the local church with his bare hands. He was quite the craftsman. I doubt there was much of anything he could not do with his hands. He could work with wood, stone, wiring, and plumbing. He did it all. And he was building a base for which God's message could get out to the surrounding villages of people. He did not know these people. At first, they were not even acquaintances. They were unknown to him, and his mission was to tell them of a God who came to this earth and died for them so they could live life with a connection to the Prince of Peace.

When Papaw preached, he left his heart and tears on the podium. As a result of his years in Central Mexico, two of my uncles married Belizean women, ladies of strength, passion, family, hard work, lessons, and principle who were sweet to the bone.

Grandma Lytle was a nurse who worked in the hospital in Belize. But this was no hospital like you and I might imagine here in the States. I've heard her talk about the dirt floors she would deliver babies on and the muddy trails she would walk home on in the dark of night with the sounds of a dangerous jungle surrounding her. And she would speak of the songs she would sing and the presence of Almighty God walking with her in the night.

Papaw was a whistler. As a child, I would listen to him challenge a local mockingbird (our Texas state bird since 1927) to a duel of song. Contrary to popular belief, the mockingbird doesn't just mimic the song of other birds. They also mimic the sounds of insects and amphibians. They may not speak, but they can certainly send a parrot packin' in shameful blush. If you have never heard a mimus polyglottos sing the morning sun into the sky, you're missing out indeed.

Papaw would sit on the porch and reel in the mockingbird with his own Italian verismo. The bird, intrigued at what he heard, would throw out the song of a bobwhite. Papaw would repeat it. The bird would skip to a few branches closer in the tree and whistle back the song of a redbird. Papaw would repeat that one. Before long, our state bird was within feet of this short Swedish American and tossing out a sparrow trill mixed with a katydid rattle, a grackle chirp, and a tree frog tweedle. Papaw didn't always win the battle, but he sent the mockingbird on his vengeful way plenty of times.

Those memories were obviously definitive of moments of peace. They were simple. They were controlled and almost enchanting. But Papaw also dealt with his own problems, his own meager moments turned chaotic. He spent months in Texas away from Grandma, who was holding down the missionary fort without him in Central America. My mother would receive letters from her from Belize while Papaw was still here in Texas, wrestling with the decision to go. Other times, when they were both here in Texas, he would yell from that same porch as he and Grandma would argue about something superficial. At times, five acres away at our home, I could hear them through the woods.

Those were not moments of peace. In fact, they really hurt me to hear them bicker. But I knew that the moment was fleeting and the hearts within them were pure and driven to find God in every situation. Their desire was to find peace in a world that groaned. Their symphony of life they would soon sing in grand coda, though it was, at the time, rough, staccato, and biting.

How often we go through life and swing from moments of bliss to junctures of distress. It is as if we hang from a tree on a hard, wooden board and sway our way through life. At times, we may feel like we're just swinging from one bad experience to the next. We should be reminded of the family in our life and the experiences we share. Use them all. The times of joy remind us that God's gifts of peace bring comfort. The bad ones remind us that this life is groaning around us in anticipation of the return of God's perfect order and majesty. And in due time, we shall prevail. Take heart in the hurt.

Friends

"Iron sharpeneth iron; so a man sharpeneth the countenance of his friend" (Prov. 27:17 KJV). We can all agree that a good friend can bring peace to your life. And sometimes even the good advice of a casual work peer or other acquaintance can generate a sense of peace in our souls when we're going through a difficult situation.

I have a great friend named Will who has been beside me since elementary school. Our thirty-year friendship has covered many chapters of my life, growing up and into a man who has his fair share of problems and trials. My buddy Will knows what true friendship is. He's "anchored." He is a Christian who knows who God is. He's a prayer. He's a singer. He's a sergeant and veteran of the sheriff's department. He's tough but kind.

On the other hand, I tend to be selfish. If I bring home

dinner to family, my first impression is that my wife should set the plates and get drinks for the kids. After all, I worked all day, paid for the meal, and brought it home. But Will shows his Christian maturity. He would set the table and then wash the dishes while making everyone in the room feel good about themselves. My friend reminds me of Christ, whom I should act more like.

When I was in high school, Will and I would ride around town in my pickup truck with absolutely nowhere to go. We would play music on the radio and sing almost every song. And we didn't just sing, we sang in harmony. It was so cool. We were also trumpet players in school. We were always battling each other for first chair trumpeter. We would usually switch off from first and second chair depending on who really got his act together and practiced hard. But whoever got first chair always gave equal respect to the other.

We also watched each other's backs. Our football team was playing in the state championship playoffs one year. It was a bitterly cold night and sleeting. We took the field at halftime to play our routine for the crowds. We approached the front of the band midway through the song, "Tiger of San Pedro." This song has dueling solos. I played my part and nailed it. I put down my trumpet. Will's went up, and as I watched him beside me from my peripheral vision, I expected an equally flawless performance.

Ten notes into his part, his lips froze. I heard a few fumbling notes and then nothing but air. I jumped into the solo at the next down measure and finished his part for him. I've been teasing him for years since that night in lighthearted jest. And I take Chap Stick wherever I go. "As a father has compassion on his children, so the Lord has compassion on those who fear Him; for He knows how we are formed, He remembers that we are dust"

(Ps. 103:13–14 NIV).

Our friendship goes well beyond great harmony and trumpet solos, broken relationships, the death of family members, job quakes, bad decisions, and the like. Will and I have a bond that is sealed in Christ. We both, like God, remember each other's frames. We are born from dust. And to dust one day we shall go. Yet we are born again in Christ. Ephesians 3:19 speaks of being filled with the fullness of God. "May you experience the love of Christ, though it is too great to understand fully. Then you will be made complete with all the fullness of life and power that comes from God." (Ephesians 3:19 NLT) Will and I know we are imperfect humans in an imperfect world living in imperfect bodies that are filled with a perfect God. And this keeps us grounded. It has brought us closer over the years, and I appreciate him and see him as a brother and not just my best friend. "There is a time for everything, and a season for every activity under the heavens. A time to love and a time to hate, a time for war and a time for peace" (Eccl. 3:1,8 NIV).

Good friends like this are hard to find. If you have even one, you should count yourself blessed. I had another good friend in my life that I grew close to over the years. We shared an apartment together after I graduated from college. We worked, hunted, fished, and even built things in my garage together. He was an all-around great guy, and we had a lot in common.

This friend of mine was not a Christian. And for years, I prayed for his salvation. I wanted him to know the same great God I had chosen in my childhood as my own Savior. I wanted him to experience God's peace and mercy in his own difficulties in life. In time, he finally accepted the Lord, and he was called into the family of Christ. And I was so happy for him.

Later on, we ended up working together. Actually, he ended up working for me. I was his boss, and I hired him into a position in a high-stress manufacturing environment. My goal at the time was to train him to grow into a higher level of employee and take on greater responsibility. But I was far more driven in business than he was. I was extremely organized and disciplined, and I had probably gotten him into a job role he wasn't ever meant to have. And as he struggled, I pressed him harder.

In the end, my friend of so many years abandoned me, left town, and started a new life that didn't have me in it. For many months, I was heartbroken over the situation. I felt like I had given him a great opportunity, and he had thrown it away. I had invested myself in his career and his soul, and he had abandoned me. And through failed attempts to contact him, I realized I was probably at fault for running him away. It was my desire to make him like me that pushed him away. God made him in His image the way he was and not in His image the way I was. I learned a difficult lesson through that time in my life, and I can only hope that my friend will forgive me and rekindle our relationship one day.

When I moved to Houston in 1998, I could not believe my eyes. Every afternoon, it seemed like the sky would cloud up and it would rain for about twenty to thirty minutes. Then the sun would come out, and everything cleared. The next day, the same routine would transpire. This went on for years. I couldn't believe how green everything was.

Last year, we experienced a drought of epic proportions in Texas. Maps of the state on the local news showed hundreds of wildfires across the Lone Star State. And in Houston, we had not seen a drop of rain in months. It was so hot with one hundred-plus temperatures day after day after day. It got to the point to where almost everything in our yard was burning up from lack of water. And my wife and I were almost to the point of depression as we had not seen rain in so long. I was ready to move to Seattle or at least fly up and spend a weekend there.

Just like with the seasons, there are times in our lives where our friends cool us in rain, and then we go through droughts. People let us down; we let down people. This also reflects our imperfection and circumstances that come along. Finding peace when you're going through life's drought cycle is difficult when you look at the charred grass of your life's lawn. The simplicity of success in those times lies with the good memories you have and the lessons you learn. This way, I have been able to cope with my own losses as I wait for the refreshing rains of spring to return.

Acquaintances

I have learned a valuable lesson about how God works in this life. It has to do with acquaintances, people we meet in our lives but never really develop a relationship or friendship with. I like to think of these people as the passers-by in our journey. They come and go like the wind. But they have a powerful effect on our lives whether we realize it or not. Not only do they test our faith in God and act as meager moments, they also act as the framework for the world around us.

So to keep me from becoming proud, I was given a thorn in my flesh, a messenger from Satan to torment me and keep me from becoming proud. Three different times I begged the Lord to take it away. Each time he said, "My grace is all you need. My power works best in weakness." So now I am glad to boast about my weaknesses, so that the power of Christ can work through me. That's why I take pleasure in my weaknesses and in the insults, hardships, persecutions, and troubles that I suffer for

Christ. For when I am weak, then I am strong. (2 Cor. 12:7–10 NLT)

About three years ago, I was going through one of the toughest points in my life. I was losing weight, I was tired all of the time, and my short-term memory was failing. I was anxious often and sleeping seldom, and I had accumulated a thirteen-point symptoms list. I was having back pains that would bring a rhino to his knees. I went through weeks of chiropractic care and days of physical therapy, and I had a stack of empty prescription bottles that I received from a pain specialist to numb my pain and help me sleep. In the end and thousands of dollars later, I was diagnosed with hyperthyroidism. My thyroid, the furnace of my body, was on overdrive. I couldn't eat enough fast enough, and my body was literally eating itself.

In time, I was able to get on medication that ultimately helped alleviate most of my symptoms, but the medication also had side effects like terrible indigestion and rash-prone skin that would make poison ivy feel like baby powder. I prayed for God to relieve me of this misery. It was affecting my job and my relationship with my wife, and if I heard someone tell me again that I was an old man, I was going to scream.

I still take medication for my thyroid problem. I used to wonder why I was enduring the hardship and spending all of the money. But now I reflect on more than the strength I gain from the hardship. It is true that, in my weakness, I am reminded to depend on God for His strength. This was lesson one for me. It keeps me meek. It reminds me of who is really strong and in control. It keeps me in check.

But this experience has also shown me the world working around me through my ordeal. I have been able to meet people I would not normally have encountered. I have encouraged people in waiting rooms who needed inspiration. I have learned more about struggle and being broke financially. I have learned what it feels like to have difficulty thinking and remembering things. I have learned what pain really is, that is, physical pain. I have hurt so bad that I could feel it in my bones. It has given me an appreciation for those in pain as well as a small taste of what our Lord endured on the cross.

My mother went through a terrible journey with breast cancer. And she came out a winner in the end. She still struggles with the side effects of medication and surgery, but she has impacted so many lives through it all. Papaw went from one operating room to the next with heart surgeries. And God used those times to work through him to reach people.

Aside from the impact we can have on people, God uses our money. Through this journey, I have spent the money I have earned at my job, so many other people— doctors, nurses, office managers, pharmacy techs, little orange bottle manufacturers, paper bag manufacturers, toll booth operators, parking lot workers, and janitors—can make money at theirs. My money has helped make the lives of other people around me better, including acquaintances and people I have never met. It is the system we live in.

I bought a new truck, and I was proud of the fact that it was a quality vehicle. And then the air-conditioning went out. If you have ever been without air-conditioning in Houston in the summer, then you can appreciate this. Even though my warranty covered the air-conditioning, I still made about five trips to the dealer, drove extra miles, and spent extra money. But I met people along the way. I was nice to people who dealt with annoying people on a daily basis. I thanked people for their help. God allowed me to experience the burden and spend my hard-earned money to support the rest of those around me who were also made in His image. "And we know that God causes everything to work together for the good of those who love God and are called according to His purpose for them" (Rom. 8:28 NLT).

We need to always remember that life will change on us. We will endure trials, experience seasons in our relationships and our experiences, and gain and lose things. But the way we choose to look at these things will determine the level of peace that we will have in our lives. God uses situations to grow us spiritually. And when we rest in Him with the knowledge that He is in control and works everything for our good, then we can be at peace. Then we can give ourselves over to be used by Him for a great good in the lives of those around us.

Dear brothers and sisters, when troubles come your way,
consider it an opportunity for great joy. For you know that
when your faith is tested, your endurance has a chance
to grow. So let it grow, for when your endurance is fully
developed, you will be perfect and complete, needing nothing.

—James 1:2–4 NLT

All Scripture is inspired by God and is useful to teach
us what is true and to make us realize what is wrong
in our lives. It corrects us when we are wrong and
teaches us to do what is right. God uses it to prepare
and equip his people to do every good work.

—2 Timothy 3:16–17 NLT

Your own ears will hear him. Right behind you
a voice will say, "This is the way you should
go," whether to the right or to the left.

—Isaiah 30:21 NLT

Chapter 4

Decision Making

Our lives are all about decision making. Our decisions result in consequences that shape the actions we enact. These consequences also thrust forward the actions of the people around us. It all works together. The law of cause and effect is always in motion. We cannot do anything to stop it. Making a decision to do something one way results in action. Making a decision to do something another way could result in a different action. Deciding to not make a decision at all and merely sit idle is actually making a decision. It's a decision not to decide. This too comes with consequences.

In everything we do in our life, we should continually recognize the presence of a living God among us who is alive and ready to assist us in our journey. When we do this, we allow Him to instill peace in our hearts for the day's trials and testing. We, as Christians, set our minds in motion for success because we know God is there to guide us by His Holy Spirit and to teach us how to respond to the decisions that will face us. And we will define success by His standard, not the pale and selfish principles of the world we live in. We set the stage early, and we keep God at the center of our day.

When I moved to Houston in 1998, I left my hometown of Austin to start a new journey in my career. I left all of my friends and family behind to follow God's call to grow the second part of my career in Houston. That was an act of faith. For the last fourteen years, I have been listening to Dr. Charles Stanley's sermons and reading his books and monthly journal, In Touch. More times than I can recall, Dr. Stanley tells of how he always starts his day with God, even before he gets out of bed in the morning. He primes the pump of his day by thanking God for another day of life and asking Him to be there in grace and mercy to guide him through what only God knows is in store for us.

Starting your day right is critical for godly success. Your new day is a new battle in a lifelong war against self, sin, and the Devil. Your new day is a battle that you will fight in your mind. It is a string of decisions that will guide you through the field of combat until the sun finally sets and you lay your head down on your pillow that night. You have to be ready for that. You have to wake with God's spiritual reveille playing in your mind.

When you begin your day with God, you make your first decision already. The first decision has been established, and it has been given over to the Lord. So you can imagine how that sits with the Lord. He starts your day with a smile.

And I am sure that He is probably responding with, "Good morning, my child."

What a wonderful start. Sounds peaceful, huh?

However, we also have to realize the reality of this, which comes with a morning of battle. When we start our mornings with God, we also kick-start the Devil's. We've also told our enemy that we intend to give our day to Almighty God. And you can expect that he doesn't like this one bit. And with that decision, we have begun the cycle. We have started our mental walk with God at our side and Satan on the attack. And trust me, the fighting will soon begin. And the decision making comes with God's call to "March!"

"In His kindness God called you to share in His eternal glory by means of Christ Jesus. So after you have suffered a little while, He will restore, support, and strengthen you, and He will place you on a firm foundation" (1 Peter 5:10 NLT).

Let's concentrate on the word "suffered" in this passage. The word used here in the Greek is "pascho," which means "to be affected, to feel, to suffer sadly, be in a bad plight." (Strong's Greek Lexicon reference G3958) This doesn't sound like a pleasant experience, does it? Jesus uses this same word in Matthew 16:21 when he describes to His disciples how He will go to Jerusalem and suffer at the hands of men and be killed. It sounds like battle to me. People suffer in battle.

Do you ever feel like you are suffering in your daily journey? Do you ever get to that point in your day where your chest is heavy and you feel like you just can't get enough breath in your lungs, like the pressures of the day are weighing on you? God designs this process to try us. It is meant to strengthen our faith in Him. It brings us to a position where we cannot count on ourselves and must then submit to the Father's strength. "Dear brothers and sisters, when troubles come your way, consider it an opportunity for great joy. For you know that when your faith is tested, your endurance has a chance to grow. So let it grow, for when your endurance is fully developed, you will be perfect and complete, needing nothing"

(James 1:2–4 NLT).

Grown endurance results in winning. The Olympics have filled the news over the past few weeks. It's that time when the world comes together to compete for the prize. We are in a life of spiritual Olympics. We are in training every day. Some of us work smart, and we toil hard. Some of us just show up and hang out on the sidelines. Unlike the sports Olympics, in the spiritual Olympics, we all try out, and we all qualify to race. But we don't all win. When we feel the heat and run with God, we develop endurance. Our gained strength results in a successful finish.

Descriptions of life packed with pressure fill the Bible. Yet Christ Himself managed to take on the greatest pressure of all when He died on the cross. He was able to do that with the peace He had within Him. This is the same peace where we can find calm within when we go through our own battles in life. The process is hard, but the pursuit is simple, and the results are amazing. And it starts with us dedicating the battle to the Lord and resting in His promises.

Dove and Peace

The other morning, I was sitting in the backyard drinking my morning cup of Joe. I'd had a long workweek of battles. Some were quick and easy victories; others were long and demanding. Some ended the same day they started; others carried over into the next. Some started weeks before and were still in progress. And through them all, I was making decisions.

As I sat there, I noticed a similar process in play that I had seen for years. But that morning, God opened it up more clearly to me. The sun was just coming up over the trees in the east. I was watching the doves fly toward me with the sunrise behind them. They would fly in over my backyard and right overhead. And with this morning routine, I knew for certain that the evening would come in reverse order. I have sat in this same chair in the evenings and watched the doves fly over my house with the sun setting in the west, and the doves would fly back toward the trees to the east. To a man of nature, things would appear simple and in order. The doves roost in the forest across from our house.

In the mornings, God's sun pops up, and the doves fly from

the trees in front to the fields out back. They spend the day eating and digesting the seed they consume. Then when the sun goes down, they fly back to the forest to roost.

This morning, I noticed something special. The sun in this scenario was always behind the dove. It was as if the sun were pushing them forward to do the things that doves must do during the day. And then it pushed them forward in the evening to usher them into a night's rest. Then, simply, they begin all over the next morning.

I believe that, when we start our day with God, we have placed Him at the center of our decisions. When we are close to Him, He actually gets behind us and pushes us forward. He yells, "March!"

As long as we stay close to Him, we can hear His Spirit speak to us, "Go left, go right, go up, go down, do this, do that, say this, and say that." When God leads the charge, we can fly through our own day and get to His blessings of seed and roost in restful peace.

Think of the successes we can obtain in a day's battle when we let God lead the charge. When our minds are on Him from the very beginning, we can have more peace about our day and make decisions with the clarity of mind that comes from having Him close. Now imagine a battle where we get out of bed, go about our business on our own, and take life head-on in our own knowledge. Can you imagine soldiers going out to battle when they decide to go without the close, precise strength of their commander? What a disastrous outcome!

I also noticed the doves' flight pattern. Doves do not typically fly straight. I mean, they do fly in a specific direction. They are going to a definite place, but they do not fly in a straight line to get there. They fly up and down and weave side to side. They fly shakily across the sky bouncing back and forth. At times, if you watch them closely, they almost look like they are just learning to fly and they might fall right out of the sky at any moment.

This is typical of our daily flight patterns. The enemy's artillery constantly attacks us. We are flying through a barrage of bullets coming from all directions. But the source of that artillery comes from two places, the enemy and us. Satan is trying to take us out. After all, we started the day dedicating it to God, not him. We also take on fire from our own self. We made our first decision of the day to serve God and not self. Everything about our flesh is warring against us. It is trying to get us to make decisions based on what we want instead of what God wants. These aspects of our day make for a shaky flight.

Doves that fly too recklessly get lost along the way. Cars hit them. They lose direction and land, and they could become prey to predators. If it's after dawn on September 1 in the Central Zone of Texas, then shotgun blasts could pop them. They have to stay focused on their direction if they have any chance of making it successfully.

For years now, our family has been driving the ten-hour journey to Florida in the summer for a week on the beach. Typically, there are between three and five vehicles on this drive. As our caravan makes it down the highway, we will move in and out of traffic. Sometimes, things get congested; other times, the road is wide open. Sometimes, we are stuck in a stressful traffic jam; other times, the road is clear, and the scenery makes for a peaceful ride, as is with life.

My father is a fast driver. I have noticed that, when he is behind me, I tend to drive faster. And the more I keep him in my rearview mirror, the quicker I tend to get to my destination. As with the dove illustration, when the sun is behind us, we will usually get pushed to our direction quicker. When we go about things on our own, we tend to get caught up in traffic, we get anxious, we maybe even get lost, and we ultimately add more risk and stress to our journey.

As we make decisions throughout our day, we need to stay close to God so we can maintain our sense of spiritual direction. We have to know going into battle that we will take on fire. We have to know that the enemy is among us, trying to take us out of the sky. We need to stay close to God and keep His Son at our backs, pushing us forward in the direction that He wants us to go. We have to make decisions in flight based on the parameters He has given us in His Word.

When we go through our day with Him first, we will experience the peace that comes from Him to withstand the pressures of life. Is it any wonder that the dove represents both peace and the Holy Spirit of God, our teacher? But its flight patterns represent our daily journey.

An almost magical peace comes from good (godly) decision making. It is indescribable. But it comes automatically when we make good decisions. We may continue to fight the battle of the day while experiencing explosions that alter our flight pattern, but a peace exists within us. Our souls are at rest, and we are assured of God's presence in our lives when we keep Him close.

Pruning

The Lord used parables in the Bible to describe things to the people about Him. He spoke of vines, branches, and trees that bore no fruit that were about to be cut to the root. Our lives are designed for pruning.

An oak tree in my backyard is full of dark green branches. To the physical eye, it looks like a normal oak tree. But if you look closer, you can see that the ends of each branch are a lighter shade of green. This is new growth. The darker color represents branches that are bigger and stronger and have made it through the tree's testing period. They have endured drought, bugs, winds, and, in some cases, fires. They are healthy and strong. The lighter green is new growth. This part of the branch is thinner, weaker, flimsier, and prone to destruction.

Our lives are the same way. If we make it through the trials of the day and live after God's will, our spiritual branches will become thicker, stronger, and sturdier. We will hold up to the winds of stress, the bugs of the Devil, and the droughts of the testing. Our faith will become stronger, and we will depend on Christ more and rely on us less. We will live with godly peace in our hearts even as we suffer in life's testing grounds.

As we make decisions in life, we will make good and bad ones. When we make good decisions, our branches grow in the right direction, and our form has symmetry. When we make bad decisions, some of our branches grow out in a direction that doesn't fit with the shape God wants us to be in. And when this happens, God prunes those branches. He brings them back to the shape and order He demands. He is continually pruning us back into the image of Christ.

When we decide to respond to the comments of others, out of pride and arrogance, God will prune us back. When I moved into management early in my career, I had an employee complain about an issue in production. In my immaturity as a manager, I felt he was wrong to complain. If he had his mind on the goal, then he would not be complaining at all. So I scolded him. The result of this poor decision did nothing more than bring enmity between us. And from that day forward, it made it very difficult for me to get good performance out of that person.

Recently, I noticed an employee who looked down. I approached him about this, and he began to complain about things in his life that were making him miserable. It was also affecting his job performance. I spent about five minutes talking to him about how God uses times like this to perfect our faith in him. Later that day, he came to my office, and we spoke for about fifteen minutes about this same thing. In the end, he thanked me several times for taking the time to respond in kindness to his situation. The fact I took the time to encourage him was paramount in his mind. And the results have shaped into a wonderful employee who is putting God first in his decision making. And his increased performance with the company clearly shows.

I believe that, when we react to life with God's perspective, we choose to make decisions based on His will, we fly ever so quickly to our destination, and we dodge the pain of His pruning shears.

We have many crepe myrtles in Houston. And every year, about the same time, you can see them go through a pruning process. Basically, they get whacked. I prune our crepes at the end of winter at the onset of spring. The trees have endured the cold and windy chills of winter. And in every occasion, they always sprout new growth from the place the shears met the bark.

When God sits on high and evaluates the details of our finished battles, I believe He develops His pruning process. We have endured the winter, and we are ready for spring pruning. If we exhibited a great deal of pride in our battle, then He prunes our arrogance. If we were careless with our money, then He takes it away. Maybe He does it through a broken vehicle or a trip to the dentist. Maybe He just gives us over to ourselves, and we spend all of it on careless and needless things. If we are mean-spirited with our responses to others, then perhaps He allows us to lose ground in that relationship. Or maybe worse, we lose that affiliation altogether.

Either way, God will prune. But the process is simply there to keep our growth on track and shaped in the image of His Son, Jesus. When we are more like Christ, then there is less to prune. As we are trimmed, we begin to yield spiritual fruit. Our impact on others begins to bring forth fruit in them. And their fruits impact others and so on. The seeds of our fruit can then spread and grow new spiritual fruit beyond anything we can see or imagine. And one day when we get to heaven, we will see and know the positive impact that our good decision making has had on others.

> Then Jesus told this story: "A man planted a fig tree in his garden and came again and again to see if there was any fruit on it, but he was always disappointed. Finally, he said to his gardener, 'I've waited three years, and there hasn't been a single fig! Cut it down. It's just taking up space in the garden.' The gardener answered, 'Sir, give it one more chance. Leave it another year, and I'll give it special attention and plenty of fertilizer. If we

get figs next year, fine. If not, then you can cut it down.'"
(Luke 13:6–9 NLT)

God puts things, experiences, and people in our lives to grow us. He prepares an environment for us to flourish in spiritually. Some consists of good times of fertilizer; others is painful pruning. But His efforts give us the best opportunity to grow and produce spiritual fruit. If we put forth the effort under His care, then we yield fruit. If we go about things our own way and make poor decisions, then the results could be dire for us. How are you doing with your decision making? Are you producing fruit for the Gardener?

Don't be selfish; don't try to impress others. Be humble, thinking of others as better than yourselves.

—Philippians 2:3 NLT

But that is the time to be careful! Beware that in your plenty you do not forget the Lord your God and disobey his commands, regulations, and decrees that I am giving you today. For when you have become full and prosperous and have built fine homes to live in, and when your flocks and herds have become very large and your silver and gold have multiplied along with everything else, be careful! Do not become proud at that time and forget the Lord your God.

—Deuteronomy 8:11–14 NLT

Pride first, then the crash, but humility is precursor to honor.

—Proverbs 18:12 The Message

Chapter 5

Selfishness and Pride

I dread this aspect of peace because I've had one of the biggest problems with this topic personally. I am a proud man. After all, I have a lot to be proud of:

- a wonderful family history full of great men and women
- the best job ever working with people to whom I have responsibility and a factory full of things to which I have control over
- the smartest, most beautiful woman in the world who married me and gave me the three greatest children in the world
- more than enough tools and toys in my home and garage to open a Sears Craftsman store and the knowledge of how to use them
- great friends and life experiences

On the surface, this description of me could come across as one from a man puffed up with pride. You might be saying,

"Well, he sure does think highly of himself!" I think there is a razor-sharp line between being proud and being puffed up with pride. In fact, I think we might do better with peace and being in accord with others if we simply reversed the order of our typical proud traits. If our focus were first on God and then on others and finally on self, we might not cross that line as often.

From my observations in general, people have this receptor of sorts that is tuned to expect other people to enact pride into conversation. It is as if, when we approach people, we expect they will have something good to say about themselves, especially if they are in a position of power or responsibility.

I have listened closely to conversation with people from all levels in business, from the janitor to the CEO. I have also paid special attention to my own conversations with these people and my own words. And I frequently find that people are proud. They say pleasing things about themselves to build up their personhood. It is as if they are trying to elevate themselves to the level of those around them that they see as "higher-ups." And in this, I am chief sinner!

I have noticed I can be in a discussion with a person who works for me and I will attempt to compare myself to him, unknowingly at times, in an area that he probably should be proud in. So what good does that do me anyway? Absolutely none whatsoever. In fact, it actually pulls the wind from his sails. It robs his moment. Maybe he is just speaking about how proud he is of his kids. So why should I use his moment to brag on my kids? Wouldn't it be more Christ-like to let him end the conversation on a high note?

In 590, Pope Gregory I streamlined the original list of monk Evagrius Ponticus (from two centuries before) and ended the infamous list with a bang, Pride. And why not? After all, Proverbs clearly showed that, in pride, we trigger doom for ourselves. "Pride goes before destruction and haughtiness before a fall" (Prov. 16:18 NLT).

The word "pride" in this passage of scripture is the Hebrew word "ga'own," which means "exaltation, majesty, excellence." (Strong's Lexicon reference H1347) And what of, say, "majesty"? We read about this in Job as he tries to describe the majesty of God.

> My heart pounds as I think of this. It trembles within me. Listen carefully to the thunder of God's voice as it rolls from His mouth. It rolls across the heavens, and His lightning flashes in every direction. Then comes the roaring of the thunder—the tremendous voice of His majesty. He does not restrain it when He speaks. God's voice is glorious in the thunder. We can't even imagine the greatness of his power. (Job 37:1–5 NLT)

These words that describe "pride" certainly don't seem to be terms I would dare describe of myself, especially because they are used to describe the Creator of the universe in which my small, dusty frame resides in. So it makes sense that, if I am puffed up with pride, then I'm headed for trouble. God is holy and majestic. And if anyone deserves the right to be proud, it is Him.

I think pride breeds selfishness. When a person becomes bigheaded about what he has, he almost assuredly will begin to think that he should have more. I call this the "deadly duo." I don't know anyone who likes to be around a selfish person. We equate selfishness to children fighting over toys and married couples quarrelling through a possible divorce. It's a side of people we just don't like. Some people are just so proud of themselves that they make us grind our teeth and squint our eyes.

Pride is destructive. And selfishness brings on more pride. But in the right order, pride can be a very powerful and positive thing. My wife praises my kids' achievements and makes sure they know she is proud of them. And when she tells them to "show Daddy," the look in her eyes is easy to interpret. She seems to express, "Be proud of them."

Our kids want to be proud, and they want us to feel the same way about them. But there is something good about pride when someone else gives it first. And there is something strengthening to us personally when we give that pride. We are training our kids to be proud of each other.

Dalton will say, "Daddy, look what Luke made!"

The detail in what Luke built with Legos is not really that

important, but the response that I give to how wonderfully made it is and the fact that Dalton was excited for Luke's creation is what is truly significant. Dalton is learning that giving Luke the spotlight is far more rewarding for his spirit. And Dalton knows that, when he gets Daddy involved, it only gets better. In harmony with his brother, Luke learns that pride received is much more enjoyable than simply being proud of one's self.

I like fishing. I have some nice fishing reels. But I have found that, when I have gone to the store to buy fishing line for one of my reels, I have left with a new rod and reel combo, along with the line for the previous reel. Why? I'm proud. I come across a new piece of gear that looks and works better than the one I started with. I've noticed that, when I'm on a boat with three other guys, I will move to a spot on the boat where I have the best access to the bait box. Why? I am selfish. Typically, these fishing trips produce less fish in my ice chest.

I don't really want to be this way; nor do I try to be this way. I have formed these actions of trends in my brain over time because of my former sin nature. The Bible tells me clearly that, when I received salvation, a new life replaced my sin nature. "This means that anyone who belongs to Christ has become a new person. The old life is gone; a new life has begun!" (2 Cor. 5:17 NLT).

Recently, I purchased a new laptop computer. I obviously took my old pictures of vacations past and put them on my new device. The new PC is much faster and more enjoyable to use. And my pictures are as clear and enjoyable to look at as they ever were. But I made sure my new operating system was revised. I replaced my old one with a newer, faster, more efficient one.

When we become Christians, we don't lose the good memories or bad ones. We don't keep the old sin nature. We get a new life in Christ. The Holy Spirit shows up and begins to help us work more quickly and efficiently through our life collection of data/patterns. He encourages us to smile at our good memories and to learn from our bad recollections. But we still have our old trends stowed away in our brains. And God still gives us a choice. With our newly revised spiritual software, we can allow the Holy Spirit to move through us and begin to correct our bad trends of pride and selfishness with godly character. But that spiritual defrag takes time. And it only works if we encourage Him to do the job.

If we continue to live like we used to, then the process halts. If we practice His commands, then we develop new patterns. When we encourage positive pride in others and minimize our own, we become less selfish, which means we begin to give more than we want to receive. And giving comes with its own rewards, which becomes yet another ingredient in peace that we will discuss later.

Struggling with Pride

I think it would be important to note that, with all sin, not just pride, we can rest in grace knowing that even the Apostle Paul had his own struggles.

> So the trouble is not with the law, for it is spiritual and good. The trouble is with me, for I am all too human, a slave to sin. I don't really understand myself, for I want to do what is right, but I don't do it. Instead, I do what I hate. But if I know that what I am doing is wrong, this shows that I agree that the law is good. So I am not the one doing wrong; it is sin living in me that does it. And I know that nothing good lives in me, that is, in my sinful nature. I want to do what is right, but I can't. I want to do what is good, but I don't. I don't want to do what is wrong, but I do it anyway. But if I do what I don't want to do, I am not really the one doing wrong; it is sin living in me that does it. I have discovered this principle of life—that when I want to do what is right, I inevitably do what is wrong. I love God's law with all my heart. But there is another power within me that is at war with my mind. This power makes me a slave to the sin that is still within me. Oh, what a miserable person I am! Who will free me from this life that is dominated by sin and death? Thank God! The answer is in Jesus Christ our Lord. (Rom. 7.14–25 NLT)

I would like to focus on a few key parts of this passage that can encourage us. "The trouble is with me, for I am all too human." How many times have you heard it said, "I'm only human"? Well, you are. And so am I. We were made from dust. Our frame is fragile. And we are born into sin thanks to our foreparents, Adam and Eve. So don't beat yourself up as you begin to reverse those patterns and retrain your mind on the things of God. As you allow the Holy Spirit to reshape your thoughts (which provoke action), fret not in your failures along the way.

"I want to do what is good, but I don't." So very often, the moment before we sin, we tell ourselves that we don't want to, and then we do. Then the moment after we sin, we want to slap ourselves for sinning. The more you practice the patterns of scripture in your life, the less often you will sin. And with pride, keep the focus on making others proud. If you give that good pride to them, you'll be better off. And as you do, others around you will catch on and do the same. It just takes time.

"But there is another power within me that is at war with my mind." Remember what I said about pride being a difficult thing for me? Satan knows that. He can't read my mind or yours. He hides in the shadows, watching us. He hears what we say, sees what we do, and knows how we act. When we do something that others commend us on and we act out in negative pride that draws attention toward us, Satan sees that. And he will attempt to orchestrate more situations that will test us in this area. He plants thoughts in your mind that lead to proud actions. He puts words in your head to say when others open up dialogue. We just have to roll over them with repetitious patterns of good. With practice, he will see that pride is no longer an area that we are weakest in.

"Thank God! The answer is in Jesus Christ our Lord." Praise God indeed. Our reprogramming is complete in Jesus Christ. Our thought patterns can be reset on the things above, and we can begin to live a life that is not filled with pride.

Disgrace in Leadership

I have spent much of my career in some form of leadership (management). I have supervised handfuls of direct labor workers and managed hundreds, managers, and engineers—those who recently graduated from college, those without degrees, those far smarter than I am, and those with much more education. I managed much older people when I was in my twenties, and I have young people who report to me now. But in every case, company I have worked, and country I have managed, negative pride lingered.

"Pride leads to disgrace, but with humility comes wisdom" (Prov. 11:2 NLT). The word "disgrace" in this passage comes from the Hebrew word qalown, which means "shame, disgrace, dishonor." (Strong's Lexicon reference H7036) A leader who wears this shameful hat of pride best beware. When dishonor is what the workers hold, all bets are off for productivity. And dishonor is a hard hurdle to overcome. You can apologize for bringing shame through pride, but it takes a long time to gain back the trust of your people.

"Don't be selfish; don't try to impress others. Be humble, thinking of others as better than yourselves. Don't look out only for your own interests, but take an interest in others, too" (Phil. 2:3–4 NLT). Early in my management years, I was extremely aggressive. I was in my late teens and early twenties, and I felt like I had something to prove to myself, my peers, my employees, and my boss. And more often than not, I found myself making the boss happy with the numbers but bringing dishonor to my employees by being so proud. I was quick to take the glory for the win while attempting to impress my boss. And workers have this ability to see through walls at the heat given off by selfishness. It's a hard lesson to learn. "The Lord detests the proud; they will surely be punished" (Prov. 16:5 NLT).

It would be bad enough if the buck stopped with the workers, but God also sees that selfishness and pride. And His Word says he "detests the proud." The King James Version says "abomination." (Proverbs 16:5 KJV) In other words, it disgusts the Lord. You can imagine what might happen in a situation where the Lord is disgusted. It just doesn't sound like a happy ending to the matter.

But when his heart and mind were puffed up with arrogance, he was brought down from his royal throne and stripped of his glory. He was driven from human society. He was given the mind of a wild animal, and he lived among the wild donkeys. He ate grass like a cow, and he was drenched with the dew of heaven, until he learned that the Most High God rules over the kingdoms of the world and appoints anyone he desires to rule over them. (Dan. 5:20–21 NLT)

King Nebuchadnezzar was really living on his high horse. He was so puffed up with pride that God not only took his throne but also his mind. At a time early in my career, I was first finding out what pride did to leadership. My achievements were going to my head. And what I thought was a step of advancement was really me being stripped of my responsibilities in management. I lost my management responsibility, and God placed me in a technical position. I spent a lot of time after that working with myself.

Sometimes, God strips us of our blessing. I believe I was made for management. And it seemed like it was taken away as soon as it was given. But I learned from that error, made the best of my new position, and took the opportunity to get very familiar with the principles of engineering, and before long, I found myself back in management. With a fresh start, a newfound respect for people, and a humble spirit, it was the beginning of great rewards to come.

There truly is power in humility. When a supervisor, manager, parent, teacher, or other type of leader can replace selfishness with a giving heart, strength is amplified. When they take pride in its infancy, that is, before it can become bad and give it away to encourage others, people band together. Teamwork is born. Inspiration births productivity. And people just feel good about themselves. That is when a leader actually leads and people follow. Big things happen when the masses unite. And pride is returned to the leader in the form that it was meant to be, dignity and honor.

Patience is not indifference; patience conveys the idea of an immensely strong rock withstanding the onslaughts.

—Oswald Chambers

In the Matter of Determination. The Spirit of Jesus is put into me by the Atonement ... God will not make me think like Jesus, I have to do it myself; I have to bring every thought into captivity to the obedience of Christ. "Abide in Me"—in intellectual matters, in money matters, in every one of the matters that make human life what it is. It is not a bandbox life.

—Oswald Chambers

No discipline is enjoyable while it is happening—it's painful! But afterward there will be a peaceful harvest of right living for those who are trained in this way.

—Hebrews 12:11 NLT

Chapter 6

Focus and Self-Discipline

In 2004, I was walking through a bookstore in the Hong Kong International Airport while on business. My eyes strolled across a book—The Toyota Way—that caught my eye. This book by Jeffrey K. Liker had a quote on the front from USA Today that read, "Toyota is as much a state of mind as it is a car company." (The Toyota Way – Jeffrey K. Liker)

I thought to myself, This is a book that I could burn a few hours on in this next flight.

To date, I don't know how many times I have read through and referenced that book in business.

The Toyota way, in its most basic description, is a philosophy of doing business that the Toyota Motor Company uses to build cars and trucks. It contains fourteen key management principles. It is no wonder that the first principle of TPS is "Long-Term Philosophy—Base your management decisions on a long-term philosophy even at the expense of short-term financial goals."

(Regarding The Toyota Production System (TPS), The Toyota Way – Jeffrey K. Liker)

Living the Christian life, in a way, is like manufacturing. We have many processes in our life that work together to make a product, our self. We are trying to take our raw materials and create the image of Christ. This is the manufacturing process of sanctification. And when we live in the image of Christ, we can expect to be at peace. And when we are at peace in this miserable, cruel, vile, and sinful world, people want to know how we got that way. Thus, it opens the door for our witness of the gospel. And our product becomes the raw material for a new product, another person becoming the image of Christ.

"Nemawashi—Japanese for making necessary arrangements; laying the groundwork." The Japanese word "nemawashi" means, "to make the necessary arrangements for something or 'laying the groundwork' for something." In like fashion, a successful Christian life, filled with peace, will take building daily character on top of solid, Christian principles; those that create peace. In a sense, "nemawashi" is sanctification. As we are transformed, through sanctification, into the image of Christ, we receive God's peace. If we are going to start really working at re-creating positive patterns in our mind to live in peace, then we need to start from the ground up. We need to make the necessary arrangements and lay the groundwork for success. We know we need to pray, read our Bible, say nice things, go to church, and tell people about Jesus, but if we don't possess an ability to be disciplined, then we're headed for problems. If we do not possess an ability to focus, then we can forget being disciplined.

I spoke of playing trumpet in high school and how my bud Willie and I were continually swapping first chair trumpeter. Why? We were operating on different levels of discipline in practicing our music. When I was disciplined and rehearsed more than he did, I would usually grab first chair. And vice versa. "Spiritual disciplines are those things that, more than likely, most of us would rather not do" (Gordon MacDonald, On Discipline). "To learn, you must love discipline; it is stupid to hate correction" (Prov. 12:1 NLT).

I didn't really like practicing trumpet. I didn't find enjoyment in doing homework. In fact, I don't really like discipline in general. It goes against my grain. I'm human. I'm selfish. I tend to be proud of what I have, but I don't want to work hard to get it. I was born lazy. I would rather be served than to serve. But as I practice the ways of our Lord, I am reshaped mentally. The Holy Spirit begins to reprogram my thought patterns. And what comes out is what went in, Jesus.

Once you have made the decision to walk in this philosophy of change, you must start taking steps to focus on God's ways and discipline yourself to practice His commands. The average man speaks twenty thousand words in a day. The average woman, it's something like thirty thousand. So if you're going to speak that many words in a day, you may want to consider where you are speaking and to whom you are speaking to. If you go to work and toil five out of seven days a week, then you can begin to narrow your conversations down to people and places. From there, you continue to divide and conquer your way into "Jesus talk."

Let's talk 80/20. For instance, in a month's time, 20 percent of your total number of bills could make up 80 percent of your total money spent; like your mortgage and your car payments alone versus all of your others; groceries, utilities, gasoline purchases, retail purchases, etc. Let's say you find out that you divide all of these places down, apply the 80/20 rule, determine you spend 80 percent of your time talking on the phone at your desk or out on the factory floor. When you are driving in your car on the way to work, you should prepare your mind for those conversations. Prep yourself for these discussions. For 20 percent of the places you go, they will contain 80 percent of your discussions. If you plan for those times and prepare yourself for positive discussion, then you have the biggest chance of having positive discussions. But the beauty in this is that, not only will it affect the phone and factory conversations, it will also impact the hallway, break room, and lunch conversations because it's 80 percent of where you talk. This too is a manufacturing/management principle.

Let's break this down into simpler terms. Let's say you spend most of your time at work on the phone. Focus on phone conversations. Before you make a call, say a quick prayer. Invite

Jesus to be on the call with you. Ask the Holy Spirit to speak through you. Ask Him to calm you and help you to speak nicely. Ask Him to show you how you can be kind to whomever you speak with. Placing calls allows you the time to prepare like that and increases your chance of success. Now, when you sit at your desk and the phone rings, very quickly train yourself to think, "Jesus, hook me up!" Now, what you have prepared your mind for when you place a call can be quickly engaged when you receive a call as well.

You will be amazed after a week of doing this how much more pleasant you will be in conversation on the phone. The first few times will likely come across as awkward. In fact, the person on the other end of the line may think so, too. But God is smiling. Don't fool yourself. He sees what you are doing, and he likes it. He will guide and help you. And your river of sanctification will flow clear and cool in your workday.

Jest

I have been working on jest. For instance, if I walked up to one of my welders at work who had recently and accidentally burned part of his shirt with a torch—I might jest with him by shaking his hand and saying, "Good morning." (with a smile) and then add, "I didn't even recognize you with your shirt not all burned up!" On the surface, jesting with someone in discussion seems lighthearted and fun. Men like to jest. When I played sports in school, that seemed to be what us

69

guys did most of all. But jest can turn bitter in a brief moment if we choose the wrong words. That's why Paul said not to talk foolishness. Instead, we are to speak about good things. When I walk up to someone in the factory, I try to train myself to speak about good things. If I'm not building that person up with my words, then I'm simply wasting an opportunity and breaking him down. There's nothing positive about jesting. But there is something strong and refreshing about encouraging words. "The generous will prosper; those who refresh others will themselves be refreshed" (Prov. 11:25 NLT).

Practice Grounding Yourself

I'm talking about discipline here. When you get out of line with something you are trying to be disciplined about, then you should learn how to ground yourself. I practice this discipline, and it works. My kids aren't quite old enough to be grounded, but I sure am.

I like the drive to work in the early morning when it is still dark. I like to hear the birds waking up and praising God for a new day. It helps set the tone. I'll drive with my windows open slightly so I can hear them as I make my way through the subdivision we live in and down the only real country route I have until I get to the city roads. The commute in the early morning is usually pretty laid back. Not too many people are on the roads yet. So why not start the day off with a peaceful drive instead of a stressful one?

When I arrive early in the morning, I try to train myself to shut my office door, read my morning devotional, and pray. Sometimes I get off track though. At times, I get these ideas on the way to work. I start strategizing as my brain wakes up. When I get to work, I want to get into those ideas and bring them into play. But if I skip that first priority, then I might ground myself for it. It's a big deal to me. If I break the rule, then I make myself pay for it. And how do I do that. The worst way I know how, I "drive the center."

When I get in Houston traffic, I like to be flexible. I like to feel free to move between lanes and route away from slower traffic and people who are obviously a hazard. Some locals would say that not having that driving habit could find you getting run over. Of course, this practice could make me a hazard. But the last thing I want to do is get in one lane and drive that same lane the whole way home. So when I find myself skipping my morning devotion, I pay the price. I make myself drive home in the center lane.

Think about it for a moment. In fact, I dare you to try it yourself. When you get off work after working a long, hard day and you are ready to get home and relax, make yourself drive in the center lane the whole way home. Ugh! But my "drive the center" principle works. I have also used this means of grounding for when I get impatient. If I have a day where I am being overly impatient, I'll make myself drive the center.

My pappy designed a tool in the clockmaking industry

that he coined "the magic center finder." The simplicity of its use almost makes industry professionals in horology (the art of making instruments for indicating time) wonder how a simple tool could actually work for the intended purpose. But it does. And so does "driving the center."

We all have things in our lives that we struggle with, some things more than others. I struggle with some things in my life that get on my last nerve. You probably do. We may refer to those things as our "secret things."

We ask ourselves, "Why did I do that again?"

Perhaps you could use this grounding means for that. I choose to ground myself for a week on those things. Try driving the center for a week.

A couple months ago, I made myself drive the center for a week for getting so impatient with the progress we were making on a work project. I was being so impatient, and I was riding my crew pretty hard. And I could see it. So, to slow myself down, I brought out the big guns. The whole week, morning and evening, I was in the center lane. You get in that center lane, and it backs up with traffic while the two on both of your sides are moving freely. It will test you. You get behind someone slow, and you will squeeze that steering wheel.

One time, I got behind someone who kept squirting his windshield with cleaner right after I washed my vehicle. Argh! But you want to talk about patient. I was so easygoing the next week that I almost didn't care if we ever finished that project.

Driving the speed limit also gets me. If you get out on a wide-open road and it's fifty-five miles per hour, you just can't help to set that cruise control on sixty. When I ground myself with this type, it's pretty brutal. And if you use it, you will notice that you're burning up the cruise control. Thirty-five, forty-five, sixty, forty-five, thirty-five, fifty-five, set, cancel, set, cancel. And when you're driving thirty-five in the morning and no one is around but your cruise control is set, whatever you did to deserve this, it is sure to be remedied.

"No discipline is enjoyable while it is happening—it's painful! But afterward there will be a peaceful harvest of right living for those who are trained in this way" (Heb. 12:11 NLT). That verse says it all. When you decide you will apply these things to your life to bring on peace, you will come up with things that are important in your day. When you determine which of those things are key to your walk, then you should consider grounding yourself when you get off track. It's painful indeed. Not only does it bring a harvest of right living, it brings a peaceful harvest of right living. And we're shooting for peace here.

Focus, Focus, Focus!

"You may feel the way you have always felt. You may desire the things that you have always desired. But the fact is, you are free. Begin now renewing your mind to this transformational truth, for you will never walk in the Spirit until you are convinced of your freedom" (Charles Stanley, The Wonderful Spirit Filled Life). "So I run with purpose in every step. I am not just shadowboxing. I discipline my body like an athlete, training it to do what it should" (1 Cor. 9:26–27 NLT).

It takes focus to discipline ourselves. You can want to do something all you want. It can be a godly thing that you are trying to do. You can try every day at doing it. But you need to focus on what you are doing in order to make it a reality. Walking with the Holy Spirit and learning of His ways as He coaches you is not enough. He wants you to prove you want to follow His lead. He wants to see you put forth the effort to focus on the skills you will need to be disciplined in your walk.

When I was diagnosed with hyperthyroidism, I lost a great deal of mental focus. My thyroid was in overdrive. My metabolism was so high that it was as if it were burning up my brain. I found things easily distracted me during the day, my short-term memory was the pits, it was hard for me to fall asleep at night, and when I was asleep, I was so barely slumbering that my dreams just hammered away left and right all night. I would wake up in the morning feeling like I had a night of dreaming instead of hours of rest.

But regardless of my condition, I knew focus was essential to mastering the things that God was teaching me. I knew I was going to have to practice focusing before I could even work on my disciplines. Perhaps you have this same medical condition or attention deficit disorder (ADD/ADHD). Maybe you just have many things going on in your life that distract you. Maybe you are drowning in a certain sin that you feel you will never be able to overcome. Whatever the case may be, you need to be able to focus to progress. The pain from focused discipline is worth it.

"Yet what we suffer now is nothing compared to the glory He will reveal to us later" (Rom. 8:18 NLT) "But as for you, be strong and courageous, for your work will be rewarded" (2 Chron. 15:7 NLT).

Fret not. You will have difficulty. Satan will do everything in his power, with every opportunity that God allows, to test you and rip you away from your task to be Christ-like in this area. When you run, the Devil will rain on your track. When you pray before that call, the person on the other end of the line will be in a bad mood. When you approach him on the production floor, he will say something negative about what you had to say that was positive. You will inevitably fail to do what you decided was a key task. And you may find that you're grounded more often than not. But keep to it. Stay strong. Your efforts will be rewarded.

When we get to heaven, all Christians will go to the judgment seat of Christ. We will be judged. Yet we will be found innocent. We will not be dealt a blow for our mishaps. We will be rewarded for our good deeds. The failures we endure as we focus on a disciplined life will not be held against us. But our successes will result in rewards. So roll with it!

So how do we focus then? At times, my office entrance seems like a revolving door. I have people who come in and out all day long. It seems that, inevitably, someone is walking in when I am trying to focus. I can't do much about that. But when nobody is there, I best take advantage of the opportunity and focus on whatever I am trying to do or think on while I have the opportunity.

I think it wise to say that, if you cannot focus on something mentally when it is quiet, then you probably can't when life is pounding down on you. One aspect of silence and solitude is focus. I'll get to that topic later in this book, but let's look at this one factor. One of the easiest ways to test your ability is to focus is this. Sit by yourself and close your eyes when:

- You are alone, and it is quiet;
- You don't have any distractions; and
- At best, it is dark (at night).

Make sure you are comfortable. Imagine you are looking at Christ sitting at the right hand of the Father. Detail is not so important. Just think and focus on that one thought.

It is likely that it won't take long before your mind wanders. Satan will most assuredly try to sidetrack you mentally with passing thoughts. If you are like me, you will think of work. Let's say you were able to focus on that concept for twenty seconds without distracting thoughts. Practice this again. Try for thirty seconds, forty-five seconds, and then a minute. Have a stopwatch or timer with you. Try to get to where you can sit down and focus on one thought or mental picture for three minutes without distraction, that is, sixty seconds for each member of the Holy Trinity.

If you can do that in this setting, then try it at work at your desk. You may not be able to help when someone walks into your office or the phone rings, but you can keep from looking at your email inbox or something else. You can focus on a task you are doing (a business quote, email or staff memo, or purchase order) and not let yourself interrupt this assignment to do something else. Practice choosing what you want to do, and focus your entire mind at doing it until it is done. And "done" can certainly be a partial done. Do things in parts. But focus wholly on the part until you are done with it.

Now start focusing in the same way in your prayer life. When you sit down to pray, don't let your thoughts wander. Focus on what you are praying about. If you are simply praising God for his blessings, then focus your thoughts on blessings. Don't mix them with prayer requests. If you are reading scriptures, focus on the words you are reading. Try your best to grasp what you are studying. Don't even try to think of ways that it might apply to real life. Real life can become a distraction and make your mind wander. Just focus on what the Word is telling you.

As you begin to set simple, specific things before you to focus on and you increase the amount of time you can stay focused on them, you will find you can focus in more pressing scenarios and more distracting environments.

My wife earned her master's degree while she was pregnant with twins. Talk about focus! She can sit at her computer focused on something while our kids are roaring around her and never say a word. Quite frankly, I don't know how she can do it. I can be in the same situation with my noise cancellation headphones on or in the other end of the house and yell out to my kids to hold it down. It's as if I am riding atop a freight train, standing backward to the wind while trying to read Shakespeare. I have zero ability to concentrate.

I think God, in His immense and ever-flowing patience, likes for us to take things down a level. I think He wants us to make things simple. We need to stop trying to take over the world and start finding one thing at a time to focus on. Then we need to practice focusing more intently. When we do, we gain discipline. When we are disciplined, we develop new patterns in our minds. When the patterns are continually of God, we gain peace. Peace gained from focused discipline leads to a better ability to forgive those who wrong us, and it allows us to walk with a clear conscience.

To err is human, to forgive, divine.

—Alexander Pope

Forgiveness is the fragrance that the violet
sheds on the heel that has crushed it.

—Mark Twain

Forgiveness is not an occasional act; it is a constant attitude.

—Dr. Martin Luther King Jr.

I am bound by the Scriptures I have quoted and my
conscience is captive to the Word of God. I cannot and I
will not recant anything, since it is neither safe nor right
to go against conscience. May God help me. Amen.

—Martin Luther

Chapter 7

Forgiveness and a Clear Conscience

I grew up in the country. We had tons of oak trees on my parents' property. At one point, we had several relatives who lived on this property, each alongside of us. My uncle's family, my mother's folks, my other uncle's family, and others lived on this compound of sorts. It was really awesome as a kid. We were free to roam. Our creativity was taken to new heights on an almost daily basis. We were tough kids. And we had fun.

On a cool, autumn Saturday, my cousin Nathan and I were sitting atop some scaffolding that my dad had erected next to the end of our two-story house. As we sat there and gazed down at the huge pile of leaves that we had raked together, it was apparent that ignorance was about to trump wisdom. No, perhaps plain ol' stupidity. There are leaps of faith, and then there are leaps of learning.

As I wiped the cold, wet post oak leaves from my face and rolled out of the now-deformed pile, it was apparent to me that this life choice was in error. I had realized that gravity was indeed one of the four fundamental interactions of nature. I had also then realized that my legs were indeed not made of springs and big piles of wet leaves were not circus nets. And I realized just then that my cousin's laugh was quite annoying. But the real lesson learned was that I should listen to my conscience more intently.

When we are young, our consciences are relatively pure. Of course, our experiences can quickly tarnish them, but in most cases, we can clearly determine right from wrong and wise from stupid. But the consequences still remain. We reap what we sow; sometimes, we plant pain. Conscience is "the inner sense of what is right or wrong in one's conduct or motives, impelling one toward right action." (source, Dictionary.com)

Having a clear conscience simply means we are in tune with good/right. It means our mind is not muddied up with bad/wrong. Obtaining and holding onto peace in your life is all but impossible if you're living a life hell-bent against your God-given conscience. We all get this miracle creation. It's not some upgraded option that we humans get. It's standard issue. It's like a steering wheel in a new car. You might get the option of automatic transmission or satellite radio when you get a new car, but you always get a steering wheel. When God made us, He gave us a conscience. Like the steering wheel in a new car, the conscience is there to guide us. It controls where we are going. You can steer straight down a highway with a steering wheel, and you can also steer right off a cliff. Such is with the conscience. It steers you toward right and away from wrong. "The conscience is our God-given personal alarm system" (Handbook for Christian Living – Dr. Charles Stanley)

If your new car is not properly maintained, you can bet it will begin to veer you in the wrong direction. Such is with the conscience. David said in Psalm 119:11 NLT, "I have hidden your word in my heart that I might not sin against you." David knew that, if he did not maintain the godly discipline of studying God's Word, his conscience would begin to wear out. And "with wear" meant sin. And David was no stranger to bad choices. David committed the sin of arrogance with his quest to count the people of Israel in 1 Chronicles 21 and he committed the sins of covetousness, adultery and murder in the account of Bathsheba in 2 Samuel 11. The conscience is meant to keep us in the right, that is, on the straight path. But if we don't maintain it or, rather, if we pollute it with sin, then we lose our grasp on the wheel of life and veer down the rocky path of sin.

Wrong Turns

I grew up attending a small church in Austin. Many of my family members attended that church, and many were musically inclined. At one point growing up, my mother played organ in our church. My grandmother played the piano, Uncle David played bass, Stephen played guitar, and Daniel led worship while I played drums. Music was always a big deal in our family. I was saved before my teen years while at church camp in the piney woods of Texas, and music was a big part of that experience.

When I graduated from high school and started college, I began to venture out into music in Austin. I started playing in local bands. Before I knew it, in the blink of an eye, I was going on the road with a band and playing drums, recording in the studio, and playing live concerts around Texas. How quickly I had moved from playing gospel music on Sunday mornings for the Lord to playing secular music in bars and clubs on Saturday nights. My conscience very quickly became numbed to where it started out. The "soul slap" it once gave me had become nothing more than a faint, distant whisper.

This may have been slightly better had my actions between performances been less worldly. But typically, that's the way things work. We act out where we meddle. When I started college, I stopped keeping up the maintenance of my soul, and my conscience just got increasingly quieter until I could barely hear it at all one day. Of course, I was certainly saved. On my worst day in the world, I was still bound for heaven, but my sin was robbing me of true life and godly peace. It was clouding my conscience, and my soul was stirred up. This cloudy soul had me driving through life like I was driving through fog on a dreary night. And it made me restless and without peace. It wasn't until I began to maintain my soul that things cleared up. I began to hear my conscience speaking to me again.

We've all made wrong turns in our lives. I've been the chief sinner at getting off the straight and narrow road that God places before me. But it's never too late to get back on track. Depending on where you have taken wrong turns, how often, and to what degree, you may find it more difficult to find your way back to the main road. I have experienced times where it was more difficult to get back on track. But eventually, you can get back to the "Christ Road." But you have to start by stopping all of the driving in circles.

"You can enter God's Kingdom only through the narrow gate. The highway to hell is broad, and its gate is wide for the many who choose that way. But the gateway to life is very narrow and the road is difficult, and only a few ever find it" (Matt. 7:13–14 NLT).

Maintaining a clear conscience comes from sinning less and obeying God more. As you focus on self-discipline in following after God's heart, you begin to redevelop these worldly patterns into godly configurations. That Christ-like repetition allows the sediment of past sins to settle at the bottom of your soul, which clears up things and allows your conscience to once again work with your mind. You begin to be less proud and harness the power of giving as you become less selfish. You start making decisions more frequently with what God wants and less for what your sin gene wants. And you then become more like the true image of God and begin to live life in the essence of peace.

Forgiveness

I have often pondered the whole topic of forgiveness. It seems as though we humans have a big problem with forgiveness. We're so selfish and proud that, when someone wrongs us, it cuts to the core of who we are. And yet again, a fine line between unforgiveness and bitterness is drawn in our souls.

The sum of the whole in scripture is forgiveness. Some would say it is love, and that could certainly be argued. But surely, love could not truly be the essence of the word without a reason to love. If a person loved someone for the sake of loving him, how true and how deep would that love be? If another person wronged someone and he still loved the other, then would not his love be more whole, more full (as we say in the country), and more deep?

God created us in His image. He made us from nothing. We would have never existed had He not created us. He loved us enough to do that. So now we exist. Okay, but if the Bible stopped there, then how deep and how special would that love really be? Imagine a scenario where the creation then falls away from the Creator. In fact, the creation runs away from the Creator and actually sins against Him. Let's say the creation even does vile things against the Creator and other members of the creation. Let's say the creation even kills other members of the creation.

And what would this logical Creator do? Destroy that creation? No, God (the Creator) chose to forgive. And forgive

He did indeed. He actually took His one and only Son and gave Him death to atone for the sins of the creation. Only the most pure sacrifice would suffice. And He loved His creation so much that He provided that sacrifice. So it seems to me that love takes on a whole new meaning with forgiveness.

I would sum things up with the following passages because I believe that peace rests beneath the banner of forgiveness. "For everyone has sinned; we all fall short of God's glorious standard" (Rom. 3:23 NLT).

We have all sinned. And we have all (as God's creation) not lived up to His perfect standard. We did in the garden. But then we fell. And we would be foolish to believe that we should die in this life and move on spiritually to live in eternity with this perfect God if we did not have a way to get there that was holy, perfect, and pure. Christ is that way (John 14:6). "Jesus told him, "I am the way, the truth, and the life. No one can come to the Father except through me." (John 14:6 NLT)

"For this is My blood of the new testament, which is shed for many for the remission of sins" (Matt. 26:28 KJV).

Jesus speaks of His new testament (or covenant) in which he has shed his blood. The Greek here is the word ekcheo, which means to "pour out" or "to distribute largely." (Strong's Greek Lexicon – reference G1632) Mel Gibson certainly did a good job in The Passion to show Jesus pouring out His blood. For the human body to only contain about six quarts of blood, to pour it out seems to be the ultimate of forgiveness from a

Son following after the will of His father. Jesus didn't just do the deed and die. He poured out the life in His body for us to atone for our sin. He was beaten, whipped, nailed to a cross, and left to hang there until He poured out his life and bled to death for you and me. And He did it willingly because of the depth of His love for us.

"Then Peter came to Him and asked, 'Lord, how often should I forgive someone who sins against me? Seven times?' 'No, not seven times,' Jesus replied, 'but seventy times seven!'" (Matt. 18:21–22 NLT).

So how are we to act when considering this eternity-changing event that took place on Mount Calvary? We are to forgive. Jesus spoke of love and forgiveness. The two work together. You cannot truly love others without forgiving. And you cannot truly love God without forgiving others. For seriously, if He loved us deeply enough to forgive us by pouring out His blood, then how could we honestly say we love others if we do not forgive them?

Peter asked if he should forgive someone seven times. Jesus told Peter to forgive seventy times seven. I have often wondered why Jesus didn't just say seven times seven. Why seventy times seven? And as customary for me, I equate that first to work. We typically encounter stress at work. And we usually spend more waking hours in the day with fellow human beings at work. So humans and stress are a great formula for sin. And with sin comes someone wronging another. Perhaps we simply say something to another person that wasn't very nice. Maybe it was actually doing something bad or just not being fair.

If we work an eight-hour workday, then that's four hundred and eighty minutes a day. Seventy times seven is four hundred and ninety. So Jesus is saying we should forgive each other so much that, if we were wronged each minute of the day and we forgave, then we would still fall short of the four hundred and ninety.

Perhaps this is just trivial, or maybe it just stands out to me, but it is indeed something to consider. Every minute of the workday still falls short of the four hundred and ninety. So how often does someone at the office get on your nerves? How often do you think wrongly of someone for hurting you, dumping on you, treating you wrongly, saying something hurtful, or stepping on your feelings? Do you forgive him once or twice? Do you forgive him at all?

Jesus was clear. He poured out His blood for you so your eternal standings with God the Father would be forever changed so you could be with Him in His glory. He passed that blessing down to you. He expects that you pass it to your fellow man/woman. Do you fall short of His standard?

Bitterness with Others

Forgiving others is hard work when your brain is not in the pattern of doing so. It is just like every other spiritual discipline.

If you're not disciplined, then it's hard to do. If you don't ground yourself for not forgiving then it's hard to forgive.

"Ground myself for not forgiving?" you might say.

Why not? Forgiveness as a human is not about doing the deed and then feeling better necessarily. Although, I believe a Christian who freely forgives and is patterned to do so will be doing it in the strength of the Holy Spirit and actually feel better. But it's more about the act of doing and moving on. You may even be able to move on but not have trust for another person. But you can still forgive.

> Forgiveness in no way requires that you trust the one you forgive. But should they finally confess and repent, you will discover a miracle in your own heart that allows you to reach out and begin to build between you a bridge of reconciliation. And sometimes—and this may seem incomprehensible to you right now—that road may even take you to the miracle of fully restored trust. (Wm. Paul Young, The Shack)

My wife and I both have at least one relationship in our lives where we've had to forgive someone for something they did to wrong us. It's two different people and two different wrongs. In the end, we have our two broken hearts. There has been no complete resolution from the situations. But we have forgiven. My wife, I believe, has taken much longer to overcome the hurt of her situation than I have with mine. But our hearts have both felt the pain of being wronged. There may never be a formal repentance from these individuals, but we have forgiven indeed.

In love for our fellow member(s) of creation and in obedience to God's commands, we forgive others. When we do not forgive, then bitterness can result. An unforgiving heart may put a damper on our peace, but the inevitable bitterness that follows will all but shut it out.

And do not bring sorrow to God's Holy Spirit by the way you live. Remember, he has identified you as his own, guaranteeing that you will be saved on the day of redemption.

Get rid of all bitterness, rage, anger, harsh words, and slander, as well as all types of evil behavior. Instead, be kind to each other, tenderhearted, forgiving one another, just as God through Christ has forgiven you. (Eph. 4:30–32 NLT)

The word Paul uses here attests to "bitter gall and extreme wickedness." Bitterness is bad news for the Christian, and it eats away at peace. Without peace, there is no joy. Without joy, there is not much of an enjoyable life, and it's certainly not fruitful for the kingdom.

We all struggle with the weeds of bitterness because we all face daily tests of forgiveness. We are tested with forgiveness because it is the backbone of God's love for us. It is the storyline of the Christian screenplay. It is the culmination of the sixty-six books of the Bible that were birthed in Genesis 3. It all comes with the fall. God made us right in the blood of Christ, and He so wants us to do the same with others.

Bitterness with Self

Bitterness can come from not forgiving ourselves. You might as well write it on the walls of your house. Place stickies on your fridge and notes in your car. Write messages on your mirror with a bar of soap. You will sin, screw up, make bad choices and poor decisions, get off track, wrong other people, and bring bad consequences upon yourself and your family that could have been prevented. But you must forgive yourself.

If you go through life feeling sorry for yourself and cannot forgive your wrong deeds, then you will unleash a river of bitterness that will never run dry. Bitterness is the water that will flood your soul and sink your happiness. "I have learned that when you harbor bitterness, happiness will dock elsewhere" (Andy Rooney).

Bitterness with God

Bitterness can also come from not "forgiving God." About thirty years ago, the oil boom in Texas was on. My dad was working as a mud logger. He would be gone from home for weeks on end. His job was in a logging unit, basically a mobile trailer (or mobile home) in the middle of thousands of south Texas land. This trailer was full of geological equipment that he used to study the mud samples that he would take from the drilling rig, the one that roared and rumbled outside his trailer around the clock. Dad used this data to plot what was transpiring beneath the earth as the drilling company drilled for oil and gas.

Things were busy back then. Dad worked twelve hours on and twelve off, and more often than not, he worked more than twelve at a time. It was tough labor. It was often far from home and the comforts that were there. As Dad's experience grew, he determined he could do this on his own. He engaged his brother to join him in this newfound idea to start their own logging company. It would not be long before Preferred Logging was born, and business was good. Dad and Uncle Mark shelled out money on equipment and built their new business. And they made money, and the family went down to the beach to hang out in RVs while the company prospered. And then came the bust.

In the early 1980s, oil was at thirty-three dollars a barrel. Most were predicting double that; some even predicted it would reach one hundred dollars. Houston was facing the reality that 70 percent of its jobs were directly or indirectly related to the oil industry. By 1983, unemployment was over 9 percent. Neighboring Beaumont's unemployment hit 14.9 percent. By 1986, the bottom would fall out, and oil would hit ten dollars a barrel. Down the road in Austin, Preferred Logging would also see the hit. And in the end, it was over. RV trips were replaced with peanut butter sandwiches and macaroni and cheese.

We had just gotten our first new vehicle that decade, and I still remember it sitting in the driveway that icy Christmas morning in 1985. It was so new and so bright. But now, my folks were probably trying to figure out how they were going to make the payments. The tow truck showed up to get our other vehicle. Dad wrote to our congressman, Jake Pickle. Times were the epitome of tough.

And they are times like these that we all face. These times bring on confusion and make us question God's plan and purpose for our lives. We question His ability to do what is right for us. And if there were ever a feeling within us that we might need to forgive God, it would be times like these. "God, you have crushed me."

The Lord does nothing to need or require our forgiveness. Let's be clear on that. But He does allow hardship, which can cause us to feel like He has wronged us. Tough times build character, endurance, and faith. And if we don't trust Him and His plans for our lives, then bitterness can build in our hearts, and we'll soon find that we are at odds with Him. The path that follows is one hundred and eighty degrees away from Him and His will, and no peace is there. The forests of bitterness are dark, cold, wet, and gloomy.

Several decades after my Dad's business failure, my own brother and I would be faced with a similar business tragedy.

And I felt those same vibes of bitterness brewing. In the 1990s, I was convinced that God had birthed a plan for a business in me. It also seemed that He was shaping things up in an almost miraculous way to align them to the favor of the business. And after many long months of hard work, lack of sleep, blood and sweat, and many dollars, the doors were open for business.

Customers came, sales rose, and smiles broadened. Life was good. My parents stood with us in a circle in the foyer of our lobby, praying over our growth and us. Dad's words were kind, and they were fitting for the moment. And we needed to hear them.

But God's full plan was hidden. The US economy would soon tank. The Dow would drop from fourteen thousand to sixty-six hundred. The private sector would gasp as the housing market would crumble and the financial sector would wither. Banks were closing doors left and right, cities were going bankrupt, and customers soon realized there were things they had to have and things they didn't need. And our business was more of an unnecessary service now.

The end was near, and the questions arose, but thankfully, we were in tune with testing and were able to hold bitterness at bay. Praise God for the testing and opportunities He gives to be tested in our faith. He reigns supreme, and He knows what is best for us. And rebound we certainly did—with more experience under our belts and tougher skin to ride on ahead.

"Hold the line," I tell my staff when they're going through trials.

Not Our Time to Sit

There were no chairs in the Jewish temple during the days when Moses sat before God, and his face had a radiant glow. Of all the furniture that God spelled out to Moses, no chair was listed. The ark, altar of incense, brazen alter, the laver, the Law, pot of manna, Aaron's rod, the lamp stand, table, curtain, and sacrificed animals sounds like a room to me, even one where a feast could take place. You could wash, lay out food, and light some candles and sweet-smelling incense. But there was nowhere to sit down.

The temple was a place to offer sacrifice for the atonement for man's sin. The priest was there to do business. He was there to do the work of setting up atonement. There was no time for resting or eating. Don't even think about sitting down. The priest was on a mission.

Jesus Christ poured out his blood, and God the Father granted us complete forgiveness through our acceptance of His great deed. Our sins have been forgotten through Christ and tossed as far as the east is from the west (Ps. 103:12). "As far as the east is from the west, so far hath he removed our transgressions from us." (Psalm 103:12 KJV) We are new creatures. The old is passed away. He makes all things new within us. His work is done with respect to His forgiveness.

"Who being the brightness of his glory, and the express image of his person, and upholding all things by the word of his power, when he had by himself purged our sins, sat down on the right hand of the Majesty on high" (Heb. 1:3 KJV).

It is complete. As Christians, we are forgiven. Let that resonate. Nothing can separate us from the love of God (Rom. 8:38–39). "And I am convinced that nothing can ever separate us from God's love. Neither death nor life, neither angels nor demons, neither our fears for today nor our worries about tomorrow—not even the powers of hell can separate us from God's love. No power in the sky above or in the earth below—indeed, nothing in all creation will ever be able to separate us from the love of God that is revealed in Christ Jesus our Lord. " (Romans 8:38-39 NLT) Jesus has sat down. He sits at the right hand of God the Father. We are forgiven. Rejoice! His work at forgiveness for you and me is complete.

But he sits and watches us. And there is no chair yet for us. Our temple of forgiveness of self and others has no chair. Our work continues. And as we continue to forgive ourselves and others, then we will develop the pattern for forgiveness. It will get easier with practice, and the Holy Spirit will continue to work through us. We will gain peace from knowing we are an example of the forgiveness that God has granted to us. And we will have joy knowing we too will be able to sit down from the worries of this life one day. When our time is up, our life is over, and we have finished our time of forgiveness, we will join Him in heaven.

"And the angel said to me, 'Write this: Blessed are those who are invited to the wedding feast of the Lamb.' And he added, 'These are true words that come from God'" (Rev. 19:9 NLT).

Jesus will welcome us to the Lamb's wedding feast. And a chair will be waiting for each of us. It will be our time to sit with the Father and the Lord. And our own work of forgiveness will be complete. And what a day that will be when we shall see our Jesus and when we look upon His face, the one who saved us by His grace.

Don't only practice your art, but force your way into its secrets, for it and knowledge can raise men to the divine.

—Ludwig van Beethoven

He believed that "we ought to give ourselves up to God, with regard both to things temporal and spiritual, and seek our satisfaction only in the fulfilling His will, whether He lead us by suffering or by consolation, for all would be equal to a soul truly resigned."

—Brother Lawrence, The Practice of the Presence of God

Chapter 8

Practicing His Presence

There is just something about practice. Nobody likes it. Everyone wants to be an expert and have it happen right now. Over the years, my employees have typically wanted to make more money, but they didn't want to put the time in to learn the skills that came with more money. My son Dalton loved his new bike until he realized that it wasn't so fun after Daddy took off the training wheels. He just wanted to ride. When I got my first guitar, I drove my dad nuts playing the E string. But how was I going to learn the blues if I didn't build one callous on one finger at a time?

Life, working with people, marriages, and patience takes practice. My wife Alice will probably tell you that I'm taking my novice lessons in patience to this day. But becoming a Christian who lives in peace and walks in joy takes practice. And by practice, I mean practicing His presence.

Peace comes when you get close to God. There is no stress in heaven. Heaven is glorious and peaceful. So the closer you can get to heaven, the closer you can get to peace. But to get closer to heaven, you have to get closer to God. And to get closer to God, you must come to Him in spirit because He is Spirit. "For God is Spirit, so those who worship him must worship in spirit and in truth" (John 4:24 NLT).

To worship God is to live with Him. When we walk in spirit with Christ, we worship Him. When we obey Him, we worship Him. When we recognize Him in our daily walk and shape our decisions on our reality that He is there with us, then we worship Him.

"For we who worship by the Spirit of God" (Phil. 3:3 NLT). The verb here for worship, latreuo, means "to render religious service or homage." (Strong's Greek Lexicon-reference G3000) Paul goes on to say that "we put no confidence in human effort. We rely on what Christ Jesus has done." "For we who worship by the Spirit of God are the ones who are truly circumcised. We rely on what Christ Jesus has done for us. We put no confidence in human effort..." (Philippians 3:3 NLT) So if we are merely resting in the Lord, then we are honoring Him. He has done all that needs to be done. We are simply in His presence. And for a man or woman with limited time on this earth to stop and rest in the presence of God, this shows honor for Him.

Mark 15:9, Acts 16:14 and 19:27 use the word sebomai, which means "to revere," which stresses the feeling of awe or devotion (according to Vines Concise Dictionary). So you can see that we're not listing out a bunch of actions or duties here. We're simply talking about basking in the presence of the Almighty. We are choosing in our humanity and our God-given free will to let God have our attention. It's hard to sin when you're concentrating on God. The Holy Spirit grabs hold of us when we come to Him of our free will. That is when His power really flows. And with that comes peace.

The Holy Spirit is always there with you. He gently whispers to your soul, calling your name. To the unsaved, He calls from outside. To the saved, He calls from within. But the calling is the same. He is drawing you near to Him. He wants your attention, love, and worship. Only from that point does He want your service. God knows your service needs to start with your relationship with Him. It only seems natural to start there. How can you help lead others to Christ unless you first have a relationship with Him? How can you teach others about His goodness unless you are first living in His goodness?

"The Holy Spirit is doing His work in your life day in and day out. He doesn't need to change a thing. What needs to change is your awareness of His presence and activity. When you know what to look for and when you look for it, you will be amazed at how real the Holy Spirit will become to you" (Charles Stanley, The Wonderful Spirit Filled Life).

We have to build within our days an awareness that God is with us in the person of His Holy Spirit. God walked in front of Moses on Mt. Horeb, and he saw His glory. The disciples saw the Lord Jesus in bodily form during His ministry. And we have the Holy Spirit. But the godly Trinity works the same and is of the same. So we should strive to act with the Spirit just as clearly as Moses and Abraham did with God and as Peter and John did with Jesus.

The Practice of the Patience of God is a small yet incredibly powerful book that describes the life of a man who lived in God's presence. Brother Lawrence (Nicolas Herman), born in 1614, became a lay brother in a monastery in Paris. He was not an educated man, yet he had a special intimacy with God that Christians today admire. He purposefully injected God and discussion with Him into every facet of his normal day. He spoke with Him as if He were right there beside Him.

Brother Lawrence said, "The time of business does not with me differ from the time of prayer; and in the noise and clatter of my kitchen, while several persons are at the same time calling for different things, I possess God in as great tranquility as if I were upon my knees at the blessed sacrament."

God expects and desires this relationship with us. To the atheist, it would seem absolutely foolish to do such a thing. But to the Christian, it is the way to God. I read the above book a couple years ago, and it really opened my eyes in new ways to the extent to which I should practice being with God. It gave me a new freedom for running my life. Having been a Christian for some thirty years, it still came across a little peculiar at first, but as I practiced His presence, I was amazed at what resulted. Not only did I receive peace, I obtained the words of others around me that inspired.

A worker of mine walked up to me one morning on the shop floor. As I customarily would do, I extended my hand, smiled, and said "Good morning!" What he said was one of the best compliments I could have ever received from another man.

He asked, "Why with all that was going on in our company— all of the changes to be more productive and grow as a team and all the stresses of the day—can you always seem to bring God into the picture and find solace in the fact that He was there in the midst of it all?"

Wow. I was shocked. But my words came quick, and I shared with him how God was there in the midst of it all. He was blessing us because He was being acknowledged as the one in charge of it all. And as good stewards of His blessings, His Word is clear that He will add what He has already granted to it. My response to him went something like this, "God is blessing us because we have acknowledged that He is the One who is in charge. As good stewards of His blessings, His Word is clear that He will add to what He has already granted to us." What an amazing testimony of God's presence and His goodness to those who practice His presence!

The saint who is intimate with Jesus will never leave impressions of himself, but only the impression that Jesus is having unhindered way, because the abyss of his nature has been satisfied by Jesus. The only impression left by such a life is that of the strong calm sanity that our Lord gives to those who are intimate with Him (Oswald Chambers, My Utmost for His Highest Impressions).

I have things in front of me in my life to remind me of where I come from and what I am made of. In my office at work, I have pictures of my family and friends on my desk, my wife's wedding picture on my credenza, clocks ticking that remind me "time flees," photos of trips around the world, and black-and-white photos of my ancestors.

My office at home is quite similar. I have more cherished items like my wall of history. On it are shelves from floor to ceiling containing things from my family. From my dad, I have his Boy Scout backpack and kerosene lantern, his framing hammer from the seventies, his baseball glove, and his leather motorcycle hat. I have Great-Grandma's pecan scale, Pappy's WWII blasting machine, and Great-Grandpa's soldering iron and wooden tape measure. I have many books of insight and so much more. Each of these items sits before me and continually reminds me of where I come from. They speak to what is important to me. They show what I am made of and what shapes me. But they are merely tangible objects that will fade with time.

Within me lives the Holy Spirit of Almighty God. And as I walk, I talk to Him. I try to make Him a part of my every day and situation. I honor Him in this. And by doing this, I remind myself of what I am spiritually made of. By practicing His presence in the trivial matters of the day, I show Him that He is important to me. And He comes out in my actions because of this. People see that. When I keep Him close, He becomes visible and tangible to others through me. I become a reflection of Jesus Christ. And it is no wonder that people would see and speak of what they see. Why? It is powerful and different from the typical pains and problems of life. It makes people wonder.

I would encourage you to do the same in both areas. Display those tangible things in your own life that make you proud. They have an effect on you and those around you. But likewise, do the same with God. Practice His presence in your waking hours. Show Him that you care to have Him around. Speak and sing to Him. Hum a song to Him. Look at His creation around you and smile. Thank Him for the rain. Thank Him when you pump your gas that you can afford it. Look at people who walk by in a store and pray to Him, asking Him to be with that person, bless him, and make Himself known to him.

When you get in this habit, you will begin to become Christ-like. And the world will notice. They will revel in the way you walk and talk. And Jesus will begin to work in your life and the lives of those around you. He will bless you, and those around you will be blessed from being around you. Your life will transform in ways that you could never imagine. And peace will flow like a river.

Wrestling with God

When it is bedtime in our house, I can see that twinkle in the eyes of my kids when they get suited up into jammies. It comes with that smirk from one side of the mouth. It's the "let's wrestle Dad" look. They hide around the corner in anxious expectation that I'll pounce at any minute. The "Daddy Monster" is on the prowl. "Like Jacob at Bethel, we would do well to wrestle with God once in a while. It can bring us His blessing" (David Egner, Praying with Confidence).

One of the strangest passages of scripture to me has always been the account in Genesis 32. While sitting in Sunday school as a child and hearing this story told, I can still see the picture cutouts of the account on the board in my class. "This left Jacob all alone in the camp, and a man came and wrestled with him until the dawn began to break" (Gen. 32:24 NLT).

Not until later in my life did I truly grasp what I believe the scenario to be. To look at this passage, we need to back up and see it in context. Jacob had just stolen his older brother Esau's birthright. And the two split on not so good terms. Time had passed, and the two were about to meet up. Only Jacob was terrified. His brother Esau was on his way to meet him with an army of four hundred men. Surely, Jacob felt anxious. He was probably stir crazy, and he paced back and forth.

Jacob could not foresee the near future; nor did he know what God had in store for him. But he certainly must have felt that things were about to get ugly. And in the midst of his anguish, what happened? The Lord Jesus showed up in bodily form and wrestled with him until daybreak. And surprisingly, Jacob hung.

Finally, after countless hours of rolling in the dust of Edom, beneath the stars of the One he wrestled with, Jacob had proven to Christ Himself that he was intent on winning. And the Lord finally whipped out the big guns and wrenched Jacob's hip out of socket. But Jacob, hobbling around by now, did not let go.

We know the story. Jacob finally convinced the Lord to bless him. And that He did. In fact, he changed his name from Jacob to Israel. Why? The Word says, "Because he fought with the Lord and with man and won." "Your name will no longer be Jacob," the man told him. "From now on you will be called Israel, because you have fought with God and with men and have won." (Genesis 32:28 NLT) Not only did Jacob wrestle with God, he had just fled from Laben. He was about to approach a seemingly very uncomfortable meeting with his estranged brother. His nerves were likely frayed.

"Then Jacob went on ahead. As he approached his brother, he bowed to the ground seven times before him. Then Esau ran to meet him and embraced him, threw his arms around his neck, and kissed him. And they both wept" (Gen. 33:3–4 NLT).

How about that for an ending? I don't wrestle with my kids too often because I don't want them to get too used to it. I try to find them if they've had a long day, if something has made them sad, or if something tough in life has distracted them from the lessons we train them up with. And when I enter into such a time with them, the energy explodes. Their strength is amazing. Their vigorous grip is not typical of a normal day. Sometimes, someone may even get hurt. We've had tears come out of our tussle sessions.

But almost certainly, the night ends with Mama breaking us up. "Okay, that's enough. Time for bed."

And they walk back to their rooms, breathing hard with maybe some scrapes or bumps. (God willing, there are no dislocated hips.) They end the night with excitement of wrestling with Daddy. They end their day with Daddy tucking them in bed, safe, warm, and secure. They are home.

"Jesus gives you this assurance. If you hang on, he'll make sure you get home" (Max Lucado, And the Angels Were Silent). I think Jesus allows our lives to get stirred up not only to test our faith but to lead us to the wrestling match. Sometimes, it is with people; other times, it is with Him spiritually. Those times bear moments of unknowns and "what ifs," and they make us tense. The road gets bumpy, and we wonder if our wheels will stay on and roll. But the Lord typically will create a finale in the moment. He'll spring from the corner of our souls and pounce. We'll get a charge from the moment, and our spiritual endorphins will rush.

His promise is that, if we hold on, he'll get us to home base. And we'll be tested and found to be in His favor. We'll have learned something new about Him and probably about ourselves. He might even let us limp away. But the fight will have been worth it. And when it's over, God always grants you peace. When you take that deep breath and exhale, an indescribable calm comes.

Wrestling with Men

Over the years, I have wrestled with people around me on spiritual matters. Every one of these people was worth the time and struggle. Why? Because Christ died for them. I have made it a point to keep them on their toes and wrestle with them. I've had groups of workers of all denominations—Baptist, Catholics, Lutherans, Mormons, Jehovah's Witnesses, Buddhists, Hindus, Muslims, and so forth.

What has amazed me more than anything is the typical finger pointing between Christian denominations. They all profess Christ as Savior. Yet they all seem to find discourse with their Christian brothers. In fact, as of recently, I have witnessed this play out more intensely than at any other time in my life. So why is this?

Jesus said, "I am the Way." "Jesus told him, "I am the way, the truth, and the life. No one can come to the Father except through me. (John 14:6 NLT) He did not say, "Man's religious detail is the way." He did not say that how you dress in church is the way. He did not spell out specifics of how you are to treat His mother or how many statues you should have in your church. He does not say if you should have a steeple on top of your church. He said, "I am the Way." So if we can agree on that then, why can't we live in harmony as Christians?

"The Book of Life does not list your denomination next to your name. Why? Because it is not the denomination that saves you. And I wonder, if there are no denominations in heaven, why do we have denominations on earth" (Max Lucado, A Gentle Thunder).

I have tried to bring groups of people together in the workplace by wrestling them spiritually. But I have done it through relationship, not religious means. I have sparked their imagination to the character of Christ and using the Word of God applied to everyday disciplines. I've seen changes in people of diverse denominations come together under the banner of teamwork and Christ-like behavior. It may not be perfect. They may still disagree on doctrines, but at least they have the basics and core down. Christ is the way. And in acting the part, I come across as a leader of men to them. And as they follow, they too become leaders.

I have witnessed some of the last people you would expect break out of their shells and lead others as Christ did. Why? I spared them the hogwash of our culture and reminded them that Christ loves them for who they are. I have shown them excitement in the seemingly dismal past that they might have and how that past is a blessing from God.

From that past, they can walk up to someone down and out and hurting and say, "I can relate! I have been there! But oh, do I have good news!"

To see the lights come on in the eyes of these people is remarkable.

When we wrestle with men (and women), we catch them in situations that allow Christ to do His best work. We become the conduit by which His grace is applied. And the outcome is usually always the same. They benefit, we are encouraged, and peace ensues.

In all of the above situations, it takes an offensive approach to practicing God's presence in our lives. We don't just stand our ground and play defense. We make plays. We get Christ involved. We encourage Him to work in our lives. The Holy Spirit is willing and able to work wonders in our lives. In every situation, big and small, we should practice and rehearse God's Spirit being right there in the midst. As we do, He will begin to do mighty things. People's lives will benefit from our obedience. And we will walk in peace knowing that Daddy (Aba Father) is proud of us as He tucks us in at the end of another chapter in our spiritual life's journey.

So it is good to wait quietly for salvation from the Lord.

Lamentations 3:26 NLT

Let all that I am wait quietly before
God, for my hope is in him.

Psalm 62:5 NLT

And when he had opened the seventh seal, there was
silence in heaven about the space of half an hour.

Revelation 8:1 KJV

And it came to pass in those days, that he went out into a
mountain to pray, and continued all night in prayer to God.

Luke 6:12 KJV

Draw near to God, and he will draw near to you.

James 4:8 ESV

Chapter 9

Silence and Solitude

Three years ago, I was meeting a friend of mine for lunch. It was a hot July afternoon, and I was enduring some heavy stress at work and in life in general. My health situation was pretty bleak due to my thyroid situation (which was, as of yet, undiagnosed). All in all, I was whipped. My friend was the executive director of the Fort Bend chapter of the Gathering of Men.

You would think this conversation would follow the lines of me leaning on a brother in Christ regarding me being tired and worn out. But it was more about me being restless concerning what I was doing in life, where I was headed, what I wanted to do, what I wanted to get involved in, how I wanted to serve God, and so forth. I expected my friend to encourage me and guide me down some specific path into leadership. After all, we had previously been through a course with the men's group director at Sugar Creek Baptist church (where I was a member) about starting small groups. We were also reviewing Dr. John

Tolson and Larry Kreider's book, The Four Priorities, which discussed a plethora of topics related to men and forming the core for leadership of small groups.

My friend sat quietly and listened. As I went on about the details that were on my mind, he continued to patiently hear me out. When I was done, his response shocked me.

He told me, "I think you need to get away and get alone with God."

"What exactly do you mean?" I replied.

He sensed I was on the verge of burnout and, though I was a leader at heart, I was losing direction in the midst of all the things going on in my life and it mixed with my physical condition. He expressed sincerely that I should consider taking a few days off, going somewhere I could be alone and just pray and meditate on God. Up until that point, I could not recall a time where I had ever done that before.

In the end, I told him, "I will think about it and pray over it."

He recommended some reading material. One of them was the book "Invitation to Solitude and Silence" by Ruth Haley Barton.

We parted. To this day, that was some of the best advice I have ever received on spiritual matters.

"But despite Jesus' instructions, the report of his power spread even faster, and vast crowds came to hear him preach and to be healed of their diseases. But Jesus often withdrew to the wilderness for prayer" (Luke 5:15–16 NLT emphasis mine).

If the Son of the Living God became worn out and pressured by the crowds, and His cure was to go away and pray with God, then surely this seemed to be the best thing I could do. After all, the crowds and stresses of life had me in a tailspin, and my aggressive work nature only poured gasoline on the fire.

Led Up

Psalm 46:10 says, "Be still and know that I am God." The Hebrew for "still" in this passage, raphah, means "to sink down, withdraw, and relax." The Hebrew for "know" here, yada, means "to perceive and know by experience." (Strong's reference H7503 and Strong's reference H3045.) "Be still, and know that I am God…" (Psalm 46:10 KJV) So the psalmist is telling us to go get alone, get down into a comfortable position, relax, and discover who God is through experience, not just at the moment.

So this is an ongoing practice. We need to do this on a continual basis. Suffice to say, as we continue to meet in secret with the Lord, we learn about Him via experience with Him. We gain insight into His will as we get quiet and listen to the Holy Spirit. This psalm is a statement. It is instruction. It precedes Psalm 46:11 KJV. "The Lord of hosts is with us; the God of Jacob is our refuge."

"Obedience to Christ's commands changes our habits and

disposition" (Charles Colson, How Now Shall We Live?) Psalm 46:10 instructs us on how to know and hear from God. And Psalm 46:11 states He is with us. The Word of the Lord says to go get quiet. Christ led by example. He even started His ministry by going out into the wilderness and getting alone with God (Matt. 4:1). "Then was Jesus led up of the Spirit into the wilderness ..." (Matthew 4:1 KJV) And scripture states that the Holy Spirit led Him into the wilderness. The King James Version says "led up," which translates "to lead or bring into a higher place."

Are you getting this? God wants us to get away with Him. He wants us to withdraw from the world and noise around us and get quiet before Him. And when we do, we are led up into a higher spiritual place, a site of peace or tranquility, a location of oneness with the Creator. Here, we can hear Him speak to our spirit and calm our busy souls.

Uh-Oh

I'm not sure if my friend had all of this in mind at the time, but his advice was right up my alley. As I began to set aside time to get quiet with God, I learned I had a big problem. My mind was a noisy, high-strung, bouncing merry-go-round of thoughts. The selfishness and pride, poor decision making, lack of focus and self-discipline, and difficulties practicing His presence, they all made for quite the mental train wreck.

It was pretty obvious from the onset that I was not prepared to get quiet before the Lord. Solitude, getting alone with God and silence and calming my thoughts, was going to take a lot of practice and getting used to. At first, I could not even keep my mind clear for fifteen seconds. It was the pits. I had work and family thoughts, and when I tried really hard, Satan would slide in some just downright evil thoughts. Does that ever happen to you?

It became clear to me after the first few rounds that Satan was not in the least bit pleased with this new initiative. The bombardment of mental attacks from the enemy was relentless. I could see that he did not want me to quiet my mind. So I knew this must be a good thing. Not only was it just good, it was powerful. So I was in for the fight.

I wrap up in and pray in a prayer blanket when I really get down to business. I tried lying in bed wrapped with my blanket, only to find myself waking three hours later. I actually fell asleep. I doubt that is what the psalmist had in mind. So I had to reestablish my position several times.

Fifteen seconds turned to a minute. This turned to three minutes. This turned to forty-five minutes of silence before God. Sometimes, I would sit in the dark after the kids were in bed with noise cancellation headphones on. I would be upright and relaxed in my office chair and meditate on Christ until I was completely overcome with His peace. If anything in this book can open the floodgates to peace, it would be this principle of silence and solitude. The key for me became a comfortable position, but one that was not too comfortable. And I had to get serious about it. I had to have consistency and focus.

Counterculture

My life was the polar opposite of meditation. Beyond the Devil trying to thwart my plans to get away with God, my own mental patterns of thinking got in the way. I had to, yet again, retrain my brain to be okay with shutting off things and getting mentally quiet.

As I sat back and evaluated my situation, it became clear that I was not the only person who was facing this life circus. All around me, there was one example after the next of people constantly giving their attention to something. Even aside from work, I could see this on my ride home. Cars everywhere, people galore, and signs were attention grabbers. There was so much distraction on my thirty-minute commute home. Billboards, men on the corner waving signs to come inside businesses, and signs on cars, distraction was everywhere. I started counting in amazement at how many people were driving and zoned into their cell phones in their cars. And right over their heads sat an electronic sign that flashed a message that read, "Up to $500 fine. Save the texting for later. It can wait."

Then I got home, and mowers were buzzing in the neighbors' yards. Kids were roaming in the house. Dinner was on the stove. The news was on the TV. And now my own cell phone was going off. Is it coincidental that all of this was going on as I was purposely evaluating things? Not at all! This is every single day.

Satan has helped create a culture of distraction and streaming information. You just cannot seem to get away from it. As I type in my study, I have email coming through in the background on my desktop. Should I just disconnect from the Internet while I work? I can't do that because some of my research and reference material is done online. We live in an information world. And it distracts us from that quiet tugging of the Holy Spirit.

Our only hope in this is to begin to define our own little countercultures. We have to ask ourselves, "What things in my life add to the distractions that pull me away from God?" Every single thing that pulls you away from a task is distraction. We have to learn to minimize those interruptions. When I get home from work, I have usually just stopped and picked up the mail. When I walk in the back door, I have trained myself to drop the mail and say hello to my family. After all, I've been gone all day. Shouldn't they take preference over the mail? But opening a couple envelopes could be Satan's perfect passage into another task like paying a bill online or reading a letter. And before you know it, another distraction has completely eliminated that golden opportunity to walk in, see the family, and embrace.

I try to get on the treadmill after that. Slow walks for extended time drains the body of stress hormones. If I sit on the couch for a quick rest, you can pretty much forget me getting on the treadmill. For distractions, we have to create a subculture in our lives by which we eliminate the things that sidetrack us from those consistent tasks we want to do or know we need to do to discipline our days to focus. And parents should begin training their kids on how to do this as well.

I recommend sitting down with a pad and pen and mentally walking through your weekday and weekend days. Write down those things that you know could distract you from the tasks that matter most. Some may be personal things that matter; others may be work related. Then get specific as it relates to creating that mind-for-Christ that you need to be in tune to His callings throughout the day.

As you begin to work at practicing focus in this area, you will allow yourself more opportunities to hear from Him. And as you answer Him more frequently, you will find that you engage His presence. As you practice your spiritual focus in those times, you will pull more peace from His coffers. And God will bless those times in ways that you could never have imagined. You will gain strength in ways that you never imagined could add up.

"Then the angel of the Lord came again and touched him and said, 'Get up and eat some more, or the journey ahead will be too much for you.' So he got up and ate and drank, and the food gave him enough strength to travel forty days and forty nights to Mount Sinai, the mountain of God" (1 Kings 19:7–8 NLT).

Silence and Solitude Sessions

"We learn to recognize God's voice just as we recognize the voice of a loved one on the other end of the phone. There is a place deep inside each of us where God's Spirit witnesses with our spirit about things that are true" (Rom. 8:16). "For his Spirit joins with our spirit to affirm that we are God's children." (Romans 8:16 NLT) "It takes experience and practice to learn to recognize the communication that goes on in that place" (Ruth Haley Barton, Invitation to Silence and Solitude).

Silence and solitude is not just a practice that happens at night in the dark or after the kids are in bed. This practice can work in many different settings. We were at my in-laws' house yesterday. My folks were staying with us for the weekend. It was a busy time from the beginning. And as we arrived for a visit, there were fifteen of us in all. In the midst of the commotion, I could hear the Lord call my name. This was not an audible calling by any sense. It was that spiritual whisper deep inside where He gets on that special frequency that nothing else in this world can transmit on. The signal is weak but clear. It travels quickly up through the soul from the heart to the brain.

He had created the opportunity for a silence and solitude session. And when He invites, I respond. No one was outside, so I walked out, closed the door behind me, walked to the corner of the yard, and sat in the swing with my bare feet in the cool grass. It was the first day of autumn. The sun was warm as it settled down on me in the swing. Birds were all around me in the trees, singing aloud. I could hear them like a ring of song around me as I sat and breathed in the air. I used the opportunity to meditate on the creation of God.

"Sing, O heavens, for the Lord has done this wondrous thing. Shout for joy, O depths of the earth! Break into song, O mountains and forests and every tree! For the Lord has redeemed Jacob and is glorified in Israel" (Isa. 44:23 NLT).

Towering pine trees were all around. This was clearly an opportunity for God to remind me that, in the midst of the noise inside, He would be praised outside. God had clearly created a world that would praise Him, no matter what. Nature was there to praise Him for His glory, whether our group of humans did or not. And yet, in the midst of the praise He was receiving outside, He still longed for me. And He called me to come here and witness His creation in song. But also that it paled in comparison to His desire for me. What a joy to know that God loves us and desires our praise so much more than the majesty of nature!

My silence and solitude session in the swing was brief. I had less than ten minutes before the world around me inevitably showed up and drew my attention away. But I have learned to recognize God's calling in these moments. They are actually quite often, and most of the time, they are brief. But ten minutes with Him can translate into hours of peace. And with practice, you can learn to hear His call. With additional practice, you can learn to fix your attention on Him and only Him during those times.

Starting Off Silent

"Before daybreak the next morning, Jesus got up and went out to an isolated place to pray" (Mark 1:35 NLT). I have also learned to get up early and get quiet with God. I try to begin with silence and short prayer. These are not usually very specific prayers. They are, more often than not, praising prayer. They are brief, short sentences.

- "Thank you, Lord."
- "Praise you, Jesus."
- "Fill me with your peace, Father."
- "Only you are worthy."
- "Know my heart, Father."
- "Minister to me, Holy Spirit."

God knows our hearts. He knows what is on our minds and what weighs on us. He knew what we would struggle with long before we ever struggled with it. So why not settle in with Romans 8:26 and let the Holy Spirit pray for you? "And the Holy Spirit helps us in our weakness. For example, we don't know what God wants us to pray for. But the Holy Spirit prays for us with groanings that cannot be expressed in words." (Romans 8:26 NLT) Just keep things simple and meditate on His greatness. He'll speak on your behalf, for He knows you inside and out. Wordy prayer in a silence and solitude session is not where you want to be. You want to be simple and quiet and give honor to God. This is the best way to start a new day, for He gave the day and He gave you your breath for that new day.

"This is the day the Lord has made. We will rejoice and be glad in it" (Ps. 118:24 NLT). "Thus says God the Lord, Who created the heavens and stretched them out, Who spread forth the earth and that which comes from it, Who gives breath to the people on it, And spirit to those who walk on it" (Isa. 42:5 NKJV). "I will sing to the Lord as long as I live. I will praise my God to my last breath!" (Ps. 104:33 NLT).

It is all but impossible for me to walk away from a disciplined time with the Lord early in the morning and not be at peace. You can bet that Satan will walk in and begin his attack to try to sidetrack us mentally after we do this. But starting with God in silence and solitude can certainly make the difference in how we react to the stresses of the day.

So don't just lean on the presence of God at the end of the day. Start your day off on the right spiritual foot and then practice His presence throughout the day. As you do, He will call you to be with Him in spiritual spurts of strength. And when you enter in with Him, you will experience His peace. And your soul will be less stirred from the stressful things of this life.

The Lord is my shepherd; I shall not want.

—Psalm 23:1 KJV

If you decide for God, living a life of God-worship, it follows that you don't fuss about what's on the table at mealtimes or whether the clothes in your closet are in fashion. There is far more to your life than the food you put in your stomach, more to your outer appearance than the clothes you hang on your body. Look at the birds, free and unfettered, not tied down to a job description, careless in the care of God. And you count far more to him than birds.

—Matthew 6:25–26 The Message

You must each decide in your heart how much to give. And don't give reluctantly or in response to pressure. "For God loves a person who gives cheerfully."

—2 Corinthians 9:7 NLT

The future starts today—not tomorrow.

—Pope John Paul II

Chapter 10

Contentment and Giving

It stands to reason that, if the Holy God of the universe who has created this wonderful, peaceful place called heaven and has given the greatest gift of all (His Son) to a fallen world, He probably wants us to give of ourselves. I dare say it is painfully difficult for a person to give if he is not content.

Over the years, I have noticed that my level of giving has matched quite well with my plane of contentment. Early in my life, I was far less content with things. I wanted more money, a newer car, more friends, a nicer apartment, and so forth. In these years, I worked very hard. I gained much but had little appetite for giving to others. I attended church less frequently, and I was not a big tither either.

As I got older, my fleshly appetite for things was still there. But I decided that I was going to work on my contentment. Trading in my vehicle every other year became less of a concern. Shopping on the weekends was no longer important. My attitude in times of lacking or loss echoed the thought, "So let it be." In these same times, I became not only a steady tither but found myself giving more offerings.

'Bring all the tithes into the storehouse so there will be enough food in my Temple. If you do,' says the Lord of Heaven's Armies, 'I will open the windows of heaven for you. I will pour out a blessing so great you won't have enough room to take it in! Try it! Put me to the test!' (Mal. 3:10 NLT)

As I honored the Lord with my money, He began to bless me even more. My career opportunities blossomed, my wages increased, things began to get paid off, and amazingly, my desire to give of myself to others increased as well. In fact, I became more interested in giving than receiving. Don't be deceived. I still battle the flesh. I'm still impatient and selfish at times, but deep inside, I long to give and help people be all they can be in this life for God. "Keep your lives free from the love of money and be content with what you have, because God has said, "Never will I leave you; never will I forsake you" (Heb. 13:5 NIV).

When Paul speaks of the Lord never leaving us, he is quoting from Deuteronomy 31:6, where God speaks His final words to Moses before he hands over leadership responsibilities to Joshua. "So be strong and courageous! Do not be afraid and do not panic before them. For the Lord your God will personally go ahead of you. He will neither fail you nor abandon you." (Deut

31:6 NLT) All the way to the end of Moses' days, God's Word is clear. He will never leave. He is always there. So if that is the case, how is it that we could never be content in this life?

I had a perfectly good reason (at least I thought) as to why I needed a new vehicle when I was eighteen years old. In fact, three vehicles later, I still thought I had a perfectly good reason to trade in the current vehicle on another one. In the end, I was not content. And the result was an undervalued vehicle, but what I owed on it by about double. My twenty thousand-dollar loan was on a truck worth about ten thousand dollars. The interest rate I had on that last vehicle was also very high because of the valuation ratio. So it resulted in a very high monthly payment and took me a long time to pay off the balance. This is all the result of malcontent thoughts.

Suffice it to say, I had little extra money to eat with and pay for gas. So giving was last on my list. "How can I give if I can't even eat?" The formula for giving must start with contentment. And being satisfied doesn't happen overnight. And typically, the results of practicing a contented life do not either. So it goes back to a choice and a decision. We are born with the choice. We need to decide to be content.

Dust to Dust

My Papaw Lytle used to repeat an old saying, "You never see a hearse pulling a U-Haul." He sure could place it on the dinner table of life when you were ready to eat. I have many memories of him sitting in his office at home flipping through books, Bibles, dictionaries, maps, and the like. He was always trying to draw a parallel between scriptural texts and the everyday life that you and I live today.

"But godliness with contentment is great gain. For we brought nothing into the world, and we can take nothing out of it. But if we have food and clothing, we will be content with that" (1 Tim. 6.6–8 NIV emphasis mine).. Paul wrote this at a time in his life when he had very little. He was likely in Rome around AD 64, and it was before his final imprisonment. He was writing to Timothy, who was taking on Paul's mantle as the next generation of preacher of the Good News. It is interesting to note here that, as Paul prepares Timothy with his wisdom, he combines contentment with godliness. He did not say that contentment is great gain. He said that godliness with contentment was great gain.

My understanding of the word "with" here is the Greek word meta, meaning "behind or after." (Strong's Greek Lexicon reference G3326) So, godliness after contentment. This simply shows that, when we decide to be content with what we are given in this life, knowing God will never leave us or forsake us, the fruit of our obedience is godliness, as if to say that contentment allows us to experience the transforming power of the Holy Spirit to give us a desire to give.

"By the sweat of your brow will you have food to eat until you return to the ground from which you were made. For you were made from dust, and to dust you will return" (Gen. 3:19 NLT).

There is no mention in Genesis 3 of a man's ability or direction to "make something out of himself" or go out and do something big in this life. I'm not disallowing the opportunity for a person to achieve great things through hard work. I'm simply relating the framework for life here. God made man from dust. He told man that he would work by the sweat of his brow in order to eat (the most basic task in life) and he would return to the dust one day.

If we could think simply enough to grasp the power of that idea, then we could see that there is truly no reason to avoid contentment in the simplest of life's givings. If we can eat, then we should be content. Anything beyond such simplicity is a blessing from the Father. And to receive in contentment and then to give it away, this is the wellspring of God's blessings.

Some of us are called to do little more than the basics in life. We are called for more humble work. Others are called to more aggressive and far-reaching work. But each of us plays a part in this life. Each of us has a mission that God wishes for us to play out. Between dust and dust, God's perfect plan calls for different men and women to handle different responsibilities based on different personalities and God-created talents (and spiritual gifts). Ours is not to compare in some demeaning way, yet to hold each other at equal levels of importance in the kingdom of Christ. "Each of you should continue to live in whatever situation the Lord has placed you, and remain as you were when God first called you" (1 Cor. 7:17 NLT).

Giving's Compound Interest

Having been in business for twenty-plus years, I can tell you with no bat of the eye that people think about and dwell on money a lot. But when you reconfigure your thoughts to not dwell on money and rather begin to be content with what you have, God begins to give you a desire to give away your money. And what father, who sees his child give money freely to others, would not desire to give his child more of the same? God is pleased when we are content, and He is thrilled when we give of what we have.

"Give, and you will receive. Your gift will return to you in full—pressed down, shaken together to make room for more, running over, and poured into your lap. The amount you give will determine the amount you get back" (Luke 6:38 NLT).

Picture the metaphor that Christ is spelling out here. When you give out of a position of contentment, your gift will return to you. But it will come back to you differently than you gave it. Picture your blessing bag. Your giving will come back as blessings that will go into your bag. They will get pressed down and shaken together. We're talking about packing it in here. And then more will come on top of that until they finally pour over the apex and over into your lap. This is a happy Father rejoicing in the obedience of His child.

When I first started working in manufacturing, I was a material handler on a night shift in a plastics plant. I had to mix all of the plastic resin for each molding machine. I had two hours to get this and other tasks done before break time because then I had to run machines to let those machine operators go to break. I would mix the plastic pellets with color and fill the material hopper on top of the machine. Then I would shake the hopper until the material would fall down and settle flat into the container. Then I would pour some more onto the top and push down the lid. Sometimes, if I put too much into the hopper, it would pour over the sides. When I read this verse from Luke, it reminds me of shaking together and pressing down those hoppers.

"We are here as men and women, not as half-fledged angels, to do the work of the world, and to do it with an infinitely greater power to stand the turmoil because we have been born from above" (Oswald Chambers, My Utmost for His Highest).

God loves to bless His children. But He partly gives to us so we will give to others. Then others can see Christ in us as we give. We become a reflection of the Father, who gave us the greatest gift of all, Jesus. Remember, sanctification is the lifelong process that God uses to shape us into the image of His Son. And in giving, we become more like Him. And He will honor that.

Giving at Home

Giving has been one of the hardest things for me to learn in my marriage. I think this has much to do with my career. I get up and see my family briefly in the morning. Sometimes, I'm on the road before they even get up. And then I work all day. I give to my employees, my boss, our customers, and our company. I am paid, and I give to the Lord. When I come home, I am tired. My first instinct is to want to lie on the couch and be given to, not to give.

It is sure to happen. My wife will want me to give when I get home. Why? It's time now to give to her and the family. Again, God's entirety in creation is giving. He made us and gave us choice and the greatest gift. So when I get home and I am in my vulnerable position, I am also in His spotlight. He gave all. What am I going to give? Only some? Only for work? What has become increasingly clearer to me over time is that my wife doesn't really ask me to give much. But I tend to act like it is the world. Why? You would think that, after practicing giving all day, I would be an expert in it. But, oh, how this often is not the case.

"Would I rather be wrong or righteous ... we must give in at impasses for the sake of God and for the sake of oneness. That's called servant leadership" (Stephen Arterburn and Fred Stoeker, Every Man's Marriage).

God says I am the leader of my family. If I can give so much of myself at work, then I should give all the more when I get home. After all, God made man, then family, and, third, work. The family (and my wife) should receive more than work. It has amazed me how, when I am content with my day and give to my family, my relationship with my wife is strong. Her demeanor is spirited. She laughs more, and I am more at peace in my home. Giving yields peace. And it stems from contentment.

My kids are no exception. I can see their closeness to me dwindle in a matter of days when I don't give them my time during the workweek. A few longer than normal business days could mean me spending less time with them in the evenings. So they do what kids do. They play together. And without Daddy on location, they use their kid brains to develop standards for themselves. Unfortunately, they do not have grown-up experiences to lean on. They haven't made my mistakes to help them fashion the best standards. And without fail, their playtime ends in bickering, hollering, fighting, whining, and maybe even someone getting hurt from too much roughhousing.

Daddy's time is important because it brings experience and wisdom to the table and keeps things flowing smoothly. And just as with our Christian walk, when we don't bring the Father into our lives, we lose focus on how He does things. And then our lives become the picture of these kids without Daddy around. So giving my time to my kids is incredibly important to the well-being of my family as a unit. Giving my time to my wife spreads the workload and shows her that I care about her and our family. And inviting God into our lives to give of His wisdom knits everything together.

Giving with Purpose

"So often when we make a gift we fail to see the way God acts in response to our giving. We do not see beyond the human gift. This 'short-sighted' view of giving keeps us from giving generously and from seeing the miracles that God does in response to our giving" (John F. DeVries). (from the book "Why Give" by John F. DeVries)

I grew up learning about tithing. My family tithes to this day. I understand the importance of tithing and the fact that God directs us to tithe. I can recall in recent years past, sitting in my office and thinking about how my wife and I had tithed above our ten percent for the year. It truly seemed almost short-sighted to me. If ten percent was God's command, then by giving ten percent, we had simply met the directive. It was close to Christmas at this time and we knew we were going to be spending more money than normal due to the holidays. But it seemed an effective way to show God our intent to give generously by adding to this, so we wrote an additional check to a specific missions work that Papaw had started decades back. This was giving "generously" and it was clear to us when we acted out on it.

Why Give?

God is all about power. He's a miracle worker. Jesus walked on water. He turned water into wine, and He sucked the water right out of the fig tree using only His words. His disciples gave Him seven loaves of bread and a few fish, and He fed thousands. There are some seventy references to His miracles in the four Gospels. The Old Testament is chock-full of God's miracles. So if giving were the greatest of things He did for us, then why wouldn't His miracles bless our contentment-rooted giving?

God is in the miracle-working business. He gives back to us when we obey. And He's not shy about working miracles in our lives. Once we have committed to living a contented life, we can better take life by the horns and deal with the punches. We can thank God in times of plenty, along with seasons of short supply. We can rest assured that He is able and willing to supply all of our needs. And when we begin to give to those around us, we leave selfishness in the dust and enter a whole new level of peace in our lives.

"To change your life, you must change the way you think. Behind everything you do is a thought. Every behavior is motivated by a belief and every action is promoted by an attitude" (Rick Warren, The Purpose Driven Life).

Peace in Christ Jesus comes in mass volumes when we develop a pattern for giving. This goes beyond just money. This means time and action. When we give and give again, we begin to develop a pattern for doing what the Lord did on the cross.

We begin to simulate His steps. While here, He gave. He came to do the will of the Father who sent Him, not His own plan. And he gave while He was here.

Our motivation for giving should be nothing more than obedience. And when we give, we create a pattern (an attitude) for giving. The more we give, the more we will want to. And the more God will bless us to give more. Few things in this life can be more bathed in God's peace than a cheerful giver. The sun rises in the east and sets in the west. It repeats itself again, and the beats of our hearts in those days are gone. Our days are numbered, and our opportunities are counted. Giving of ourselves can assure us of a life of peace, and our giving measures the amount of that peace. The actions that we enact become the quest for Christ. This spiritual voyage truly is the pursuit of peace.

Pursuing Peace – Appendix A
Scriptures referenced by Chapter

Foreward

Acts 17:27

Chapter 1

Genesis 1:2

Genesis 1:1

Genesis 1:31

Genesis 2:17

Psalm 51:5

Romans 5:12

Ecclesiastes 9:11

Chapter 2

Genesis 1:27

Genesis 2:7

Genesis 2:21-22

Philippians 4:6-7

Deuteronomy 29:29

John 14:26-27

Revelation 1:12-17

Romans 8:20-23

Chapter 3

Isaiah 52:7

Proverbs 27:17

Ephesians 3:19

Ecclesiastes 3:19

Ecclesiastes 3:1

2 Corinthians 12:7-10

Romans 8:28

Chapter 4

James 1:1-2

2 Timothy 3:16-17

Isaiah 30:21

1 Peter 5:10

Matthew 16:21

James 1:1-2

Luke 13:6-9

Chapter 5

Deuteronomy 8:11-14

Proverbs 18:12

Proverbs 16:18

Job 37:1-5

2 Corinthians 5:17

Romans 7:14-25

Proverbs 11:2

Philippians 2:3-4

Proverbs 16:5

Daniel 5:20-21

Chapter 6

Proverbs 12:1

Proverbs 11:25

Hebrews 12:11

1 Corinthians 9:26-27

Romans 8:18

2 Corinthians 15:7

Chapter 7

Psalms 119:11

Matthew 7:13-14

Romans 3:23

John 14:6

Matthew 26:28

Matthew 18:21-22

Acts 8:4-25

Ephesians 4:30-32

Psalms 103:12

Hebrews 1:3

Romans 8:38-39

Revelation 19:9

Chapter 8

John 4:24

Philippians 3:3

Mark 15:9

Acts 16:14

Acts 19:27

Genesis 32:24

Genesis 33:3-4

Chapter 9

Lamentations 3:26

Psalm 62:5

Revelation 8:1

Luke 6:12

James 4:8

Luke 5:15-16

Psalm 46:10,11

Matthew 4:1

I Kings 19:7-8

Romans 8:16

Romans 8:26

Mark 1:35

Psalm 118:24

Isaiah 42:5

Psalm 104:33

Chapter 10

Psalm 23:1

Matthew 6:25-26

2 Corinthians 9:7

Malachi 3:10

Hebrews 13:5

Luke 6:38

Deuteronomy 31:6

1 Timothy 6:6-8

Genesis 3:19

1 Corinthians 7:17

Luke 6:38

About the Author

J.E. HUCKABEE is a business executive from Texas. He has worked in manufacturing for over twenty years and managed factories in America and in other countries around the globe. Jason is educated in electrical engineering but thrives in business management and personnel leadership. Pursuing Peace is his first book. A Christian for over thirty years, Jason has personally experienced the joys and hardships of life with Christ at his side. He has also experienced like times in the lives of those around him. Th e link between the two has been the quest for inner peace. Jason began to notice this commonality between people. He then joined his life experiences with God's Word to write Pursing Peace as a simple means for growing peace in the minds and hearts of people.

Jason lives in Houston, Texas, with his wife, Alice, and their three children. Th ey are members of Sugar Creek Baptist Church in Sugar Land. Jason enjoys ministering to his men's group at work. He likes to repair antique clocks, make exotic wood writing instruments, and spends hours at a time tinkering in the garage or just being in the great outdoors.

Visit Jason's website at JEHuckabee.com.

Made in the USA
Middletown, DE
18 February 2017